EGYPT IN THE AGE OF THE PYRAMIDS

GUILLEMETTE ANDREU

EGYPT

IN THE AGE OF THE PYRAMIDS

Translated from the French by David Lorton

CORNELL UNIVERSITY PRESS *Ithaca & London*

The publisher gratefully acknowledges the assistance of the French Ministry of Culture in defraying part of the cost of translation.

Originally published as *L'Égypte au temps des pyramides: Troisième millénaire avant J.-C.,* © Hachette Livre, Département Hachette référence, 1994.

First published 1997 by Cornell University Press

First printing, Cornell Paperbacks, 1997

Printed in the United States of America

⊚The paper in this book meets the minimum requirements of the American National Standard for Information Sciences—Permanence of Paper for Printed Library Materials, ANSI Z39.48-1984.

Cloth printing

10 9 8 7 6 5 4 3 2 1

Paperback printing

10 9 8 7 6 5 4 3 2 1

Library of Congress Cataloging-in-Publication Data

Andreu, Guillemette.

[L'Égypte au temps des pyramides. English]

Egypt in the age of the pyramids / Guillemette Andreu ; David Lorton, translator.

p.   cm.

Includes bibliographical references (p.   ) and indexes.

ISBN 0-8014-3222-7 (cloth : alk. paper)

ISBN 0-8014-8313-1 (pbk. : alk. paper)

1. Egypt—Civilization—To 332 B.C.

DT61.A6313   1997

932—dc21   96-48461

TO MY PARENTS

CONTENTS

ACKNOWLEDGMENTS

Béatrix Midant-Reynes, who is a specialist in Egyptian prehistory, furnished information on this period which I have used in the first chapter. Henri and Jeanne Lanoë assisted me throughout the writing of the book. May they find here a fond expression of my gratitude.

Finally, with regard to this English translation, David Lorton agreed to lend his knowledge and his talent to this edition. I am very grateful to him.

G. A.

ACKNOWLEDGMENTS

TRANSLATOR'S NOTE

In this book, the following conventions have been followed in the citations from ancient Egyptian texts:

Parentheses ( ) enclose words or brief explanations that have been added for clarity.

Square brackets [ ] enclose words that have been restored in a lacuna.

An ellipsis . . . indicates that a word or words in the original text have been omitted in the citation.

An ellipsis in square brackets [. . .] indicates that a word or words in a lacuna have not been restored.

English-speaking Egyptologists have no single set of conventions for the rendering of ancient Egyptian and modern Arabic personal and place names. Most of the names mentioned in this book occur in a standard reference work, John Baines and Jaromír Málek, *Atlas of Ancient Egypt* (New York: Facts on File, 1980), and the renderings here follow those in that volume. The only exception is the omission of the typographical sign for *ayin;* this consonant does not exist in English, and it was felt that its inclusion would serve only as a distraction to the reader. Significant variant renderings are noted in the General Index.

Guillemette Andreu's book is a warm and vivid introduction to the topic of life in ancient Egypt, and I feel honored to have been asked by Cornell University Press to serve as its translator. It gives me great pleasure to acknowledge here those who graciously gave of their time to ease the burden of my task: the author herself, who answered my many questions with patience and good humor; Dr. Eckhard Eichler; Dr. John W. Wells; and Mrs. Marinette Rosenfeld.

D. L.

The Great Sphinx at Giza. Photo by Sune Ericsson.

CHRONOLOGY

3150–2700	THINITE PERIOD First and Second Dynasties.
2700–2200	OLD KINGDOM Beginning of the Age of the Pyramids.
2700–2625	Third Dynasty. Capital at Memphis. Reign of Djoser.
2625–2510	Fourth Dynasty. Reigns of Snofru, Khufu, Radjedef, Khephren, Menkaure.
2510–2460	Fifth Dynasty. Reigns of Userkaf, Izezi, and Wenis.
2460–2200	Sixth Dynasty. Reigns of Pepy I and Pepy II.
2200–2060	FIRST INTERMEDIATE PERIOD Seventh to Eleventh Dynasties.
2060–1635	MIDDLE KINGDOM
2061	Victory of Mentuhotpe II, fifth king of the Eleventh Dynasty, and reunification of Egypt.
2060–1991	End of the Eleventh Dynasty.
1991–1785	Twelfth Dynasty. Capital at el-Lisht. Kings named Amenemhet and Senwosret.
1785–1635	Thirteenth Dynasty.
	END OF THE AGE OF THE PYRAMIDS
1635–1580	SECOND INTERMEDIATE PERIOD Occupation of Egypt by the Hyksos. Capital at Avaris in the delta.
1552–1070	NEW KINGDOM

N.B.: The dates given above concern the earliest periods of pharaonic history and are approximate. Ongoing research will undoubtedly modify some of them by about ten or twenty years.

EGYPT
IN THE
AGE OF
THE
PYRAMIDS

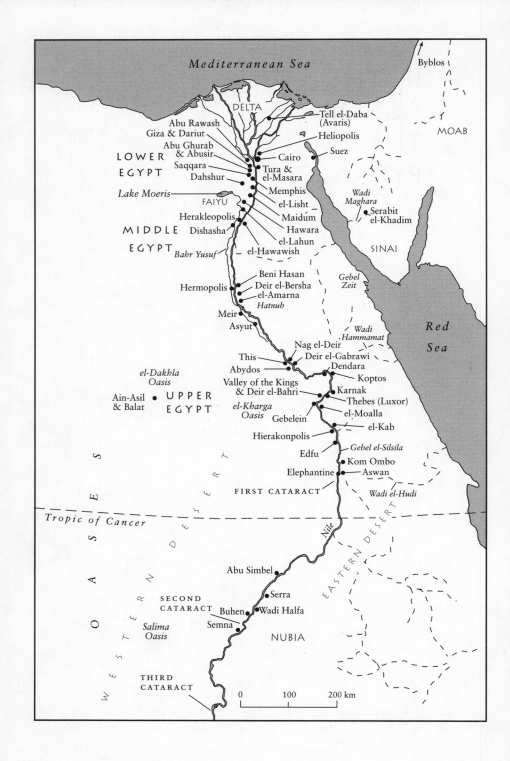

Mediterranean Sea

DELTA

Byblos

MOAB

Abu Rawash
Giza & Dariut
Abu Ghurab & Abusir
Saqqara
Dahshur

Cairo

Heliopolis

Suez

LOWER
EGYPT

Tura & el-Masara

Memphis

Wadi Maghara

Serabit el-Khadim

Lake Moeris

FAIYU

el-Lisht

Herakleopolis

Dishasha

MIDDLE
EGYPT

Bahr Yusuf

Maidum

Hawara

el-Lahun

el-Hawawish

SINAI

Beni Hasan

Deir el-Bersha

el-Amarna

Hatnub

Hermopolis

Gebel Zeit

Meir

Asyut

Nag el-Deir

Wadi Hammamat

Red
Sea

el-Dakhla
Oasis

This

Abydos

Deir el-Gabrawi

Dendara

Koptos

Ain-Asil
& Balat

UPPER
EGYPT

Valley of the Kings
& Deir el-Bahri

Karnak

Thebes (Luxor)

el-Kharga
Oasis

Gebelein

el-Moalla

el-Kab

Hierakonpolis

Edfu

Gebel el-Silsila

Kom Ombo

Elephantine

Aswan

FIRST CATARACT

Wadi el-Hudi

Tropic of Cancer

Nile

EASTERN DESERT

WESTERN DESERT

Abu Simbel

Serra

SECOND
CATARACT

Buhen

Wadi Halfa

Salima
Oasis

Semna

NUBIA

THIRD
CATARACT

0   100   200 km

1 THE AGE OF THE PYRAMIDS

The age of the pyramids was one of the earliest epochs of pharaonic civilization. It began around 2700 B.C.E. and ended about 1750, thus lasting nearly a millennium and corresponding to what modern historians call the Old Kingdom and the Middle Kingdom. A connecting thread running through the whole period is the custom by which pharaohs were buried: their tombs were enormous pyramids of stone strewn through the deserts like so many symbols of universal power. Moreover, for the Egyptians of succeeding eras, this dawn of pharaonic Egypt did not signify the infancy of their ancient civilization. Quite the contrary, it marked a Golden Age that would remain in their memory as both an apogee and a model.

HISTORICAL SUMMARY

The pharaonic system was in place by about 3000 B.C.E., in what is called the Thinite Period. By divine right, the monarch governed the "Two Lands," the designation of Upper and Lower Egypt united under his authority. His administration began to organize agricultural activities, managing the irrigation of the fields and keeping the canals in good repair. By way of picture-signs inspired by the animals and plants on the banks of the Nile, writing developed to facilitate the exercise of power. In the various locales, in the confines of the sanctuaries, priests made offerings to the many deities whose benevolent actions made it possible to maintain the cosmic order and avoid a return to chaos.

The population of Egypt began to take form as a social group composed of farmers and artisans. This society was gathered in villages on both sides of the Nile and lived by hunting and gathering, fishing, agriculture, and animal husbandry. Clusters of such settlements grew up, located on ground higher than the Nile floodplain, yet close to the cultivated fields. The exploitation of the inundation was under way, prompted by the necessity of feeding an ever increasing population.

Stretching 630 miles between the Mediterranean Sea and the African interior, Egypt was from the beginning cradle to a heterogeneous population, one whose diverse characteristics stemmed from several migrations that occurred during the fourth millennium. The blending of ethnic traits ultimately resulted in a remarkable Egyptian "type" that is especially well illustrated in pharaonic statuary. The portraits created by Egyptian sculptors represent a people of medium stature, with a light skin that could be tanned by the blazing sun, and with nonnegroid features. Their hair was black and straight, sometimes wavy, though never tightly curled. Closer to the heart of Africa, of course, characteristically black African features became more and more predominant, owing to the natural influence of geographic context.

Beginning in the fourth millennium, an increasingly coordinated agriculture came to replace an economy based on hunting and gathering. Between 3000 and 1750, the Nile valley experienced a considerable growth in population. The population in 3000 B.C.E. has been estimated at 850,000; by 1800 it reached nearly 2 million. These Egyptians lived in the floodplain itself, and the areas of greatest population density were those between Aswan and Koptos in Upper Egypt, and between the Faiyum and the southern tip of the delta in Lower Egypt. Until a very late period, the areas close to the Mediterranean attracted only a small population; moreover, the essentially Nilotic character of the Egyptians was one of their enduring traits. The sea was gateway to the terrifying unknown, while the delta was a vast swamp whose fringes were reserved for herdsmen; only its central part had a sedentary population. The scarcity of sources of drinking water was one of the factors that made this area of scant attraction. Given these conditions, one can estimate the surface area of Egypt in the age of the pyramids as nearly 3,100 square miles.

THE LIFE-GIVING NILE

The inundation was a natural phenomenon that swelled the Nile with rainwater from monsoons in Ethiopia. It came every year in mid-July and covered the floodplain with water nearly five feet deep. By autumn, when the Nile receded into the riverbed, the inundation had deposited a rich silt over the alluvial land. It was this silt that permitted an extensive agriculture, a prosperous economy, and a way of life that was uniquely Egyptian to thrive.

A wet period had endowed Egypt's climate with a light yet dependable rainfall. From the beginning of the third millennium on, however, the rainfall gradually diminished, giving way to an aridity like that of today. For the most part, the sun shone brightly every day, and in any given year, only the rare shower or storm darkened the sky for a few hours. Such events were viewed as dangerous manifestations of wicked forces, and the return of sunshine marked the victory of good over evil.

At a very early date, the Egyptians worked out a calendar based on a year of 365 days, divided into twelve lunar months. The organization of a system of taxation to fill the state storehouses punctually had made a calendar necessary, and thanks to the regular return of the Nile inundation and astronomical observations, the Egyptians were able to arrive at one. Their New Year's Day coincided with the heliacal rising of the Dog Star, our Sirius: each year, this star reappeared in the eastern sky at sunrise around July 19, which was also when the first swelling of the inundation occurred.

The three great agricultural phases of the land, as regulated by the river's inundation, gave the seasons their names. The first was the "Inundation" (*akhet*) that covered the fields from mid-July to mid-November, bringing life-giving water at the hottest time of the year. Next came the season of "Emergence" (*peret*), that is to say, the return of the river to its bed and the emergence of the waterlogged land. It was during this season, from mid-November to mid-March, that the farmers worked in the fields. From mid-March to mid-July, there was "Dryness" (*shemu*), marking the end of the harvest, when the parched soil cracked and the river was at its lowest level.

THE BIRTH OF WRITING

At an early date, the need for a system of written notation to record dates and events, calculations, or even good stories was apparent. The hieroglyphic writing system thus began to develop at the same time that pharaonic civilization was born. Incorrectly called "hieroglyphs" (sacred writing) by the Greeks, the signs employed were pictures whose shapes designated concrete realities in the Egyptian environment: animals, plants, buildings, tools, furniture, and of course, human beings and deities. For example, if the text to be written contained the words "cat" and "child," one could draw a cat or a child. But an ideographic system failed when it came to expressing abstract concepts, such as "to think," "to love," or "to be sad." This difficulty was overcome by the use of the same ideograms, not for what they pictured, but for their phonetic values. Thus, the sign for "eye" (pronounced *ir*) is found as an ideogram in the word for "eye" and enters into the composition of the word *irtyw* ("blue") as a phonogram. Various graphic tools were employed to distinguish between homonyms and homophones. Actual ideograms were usually followed by a vertical stroke. When a word was written with several phonograms, it could be read with the help of "determinatives," which were placed at the end of a word to indicate the semantic category to which it belonged. Thus all the actions of the sun (rising, shining, setting), ideas of time, and the divisions of time were "determined" by the pictogram of the sun disk.

Such subtleties, when used in combination, enabled Egyptians to write some of the most beautiful texts in the literary heritage of humankind. In 1822, Jean-François Champollion succeeded in understanding them, thus allowing the scribes of ancient Egypt to speak once again. By deciphering the hieroglyphic writing system, Champollion gave birth to the field of Egyptology, which studies, with rigor and precision, all aspects of pharaonic civilization, dividing it into various specialties: archaeology, epigraphy, linguistics, history, art history, the theology of local cults, anthropology of religion, and so on. The beautiful art and architecture of ancient Egypt and the seemingly mysterious hieroglyphs that cover them have prompted many in western lands to become Egyptologists. Even in ancient times, Egypt fascinated the Greeks when they discovered it in the wake of Alexander the Great in the fourth century B.C.E. Several Egyptian words have come down through Greek into our own language: *ebony*, *gum*, *sack*, *ibis*, *oasis*, *basalt*, and *alabaster* are scarcely altered phonetic transcriptions of original Egyptian words.

Ancient Egyptian is in part related to the Semitic languages, and it shares some characteristics with them, in particular a consonantal writing system: vowels are not written in the hieroglyphic texts, which makes it very difficult to reconstruct how words were actually pronounced. We are equally uninformed about which syllables were accented, how changes in accent affected the pronunciation, and regional dialects, which must have differed markedly in a country stretching 630 miles from north to south. Spoken and written for more than three thousand years, this language underwent an ongoing evolution that has been well traced by linguists. About 2000 B.C.E., there were approximately seven hundred hieroglyphic signs; at the beginning of the Christian era, we find nearly five thousand, with variant forms and multiple sound values.

Over the course of the age of the pyramids, the archaic language of the Old Kingdom developed into the classical form of the Middle Kingdom. Year by year, Egyptologists draw closer to the meaning of the texts and thus penetrate more intimately into ancient Egyptian thought. Present-day studies strongly stress that the scribes and those who decorated the temples and tombs constantly indulged in graphic word plays: it was an absolute rule that text and image not only correspond but even blend into one another. Thus, in reading the scenes from pharaonic monuments, one cannot stop with the mere decipherment of the hieroglyphs carved on the walls. Generally, it was on the walls of the mastabas (private tombs of the Old Kingdom) that this double level of writing and reading reached its most remarkable and sophisticated stage.

THE PREDYNASTIC ERA

By about 3200 B.C.E., everything was in place for Egypt to make her entry into history and for pharaonic order to reign supreme on the banks of the Nile. The reigns of the earliest pharaohs, who constituted the First Dynasty, began at that time. This "emergence" was in fact the culmination of a slow evolution that began about 300,000, with the Lower Paleolithic era. The earliest traces of group settlements and an abundant stone tool industry bear witness to this lengthy period. The successive cultures in the Nile valley down to the fourth millennium (the "predynastic" period) displayed an ever stronger mastery of the techniques of hunting and gathering, fishing, and the domestication of wild species. The ceramic and lithic industries — that is, vases and palettes of hard stone — exhibited a dazzling skill and artistic sense (Figure 1). Between 3500 and 3200, Upper and Lower Egypt were in such close contact that the differences in their cultures rapidly diminished, presaging the political unity that lay ahead. Hieroglyphs appeared on funerary stelae, and the first traces of religious thought emerged. At predynastic sites — mostly cemeteries — tombs richly endowed with funerary goods have been found, revealing practices undoubtedly intended to combat the forces of the hereafter. Nearby animal burials, sometimes

accompanied by offerings intended to help the creature survive, imitate those of humans. Surely we may see in this practice the beginning of the animal cults, one of the distinctive features of Egyptian religion.

THE DYNASTIES

Manetho, an Egyptian priest and scholar under kings Ptolemy I and Ptolemy II (third century B.C.E.), made the first attempt to write a history of Egypt, dividing it into thirty-one dynasties. This classification is still maintained by modern historians, who also follow their ancient ancestor in calling the first two dynasties "Thinite," after the name of the town of This, near Abydos in Upper Egypt. In fact, the tombs of the kings of these two dynasties, dating to between 3150 and 2700, were discovered in the cemetery of Abydos. The founding of the city of Memphis, modern Saqqara, dates to this period. Contemporary documents provide early evidence for the cults of major deities of the Egyptian pantheon: Re, Horus, Seth, Osiris, Anubis, Sokar, and the crocodile god Sobek. Beyond their borders, the Egyptians waged war with neighboring peoples to the south and the west; expeditions to Sinai defeated Bedouins and brought back turquoise. In this early era, royal succession was already from father to son, and kings celebrated their jubilees (called *sed*-festivals) and alternately wore the regalia of Upper and Lower Egypt. At the end of the Second Dynasty, the pharaonic monarchy controlled both the north and the south of the country, and Memphis was proclaimed the political capital, at the expense of Abydos.

THE OLD KINGDOM

The Old Kingdom (2700–2200 B.C.E.), which inaugurated the age of the pyramids, began with the Third Dynasty (2700–2625), which was dominated by the reign of Djoser. His famous pyramid at Saqqara symbolizes his ambition and power. Aided in his projects by his no less celebrated architect Imhotep, he conceived the idea of being buried in an immense monument of stone, which was to assume the form of a pyramid, a sort of gigantic, monumental stairway that would enable the deceased pharaoh to enter the realm of the sun and the sky and meet his peers, the gods. Egypt made great technical and scientific advances, thanks to the genius and inventiveness of Imhotep: in later ages, he was deified as the patron saint of scholars. What we know of religious thought, from this period on, reveals an immanent concept of the divine, a living physical force of nature which governed the cosmic order.

The Fourth Dynasty (2625–2510 B.C.E.) began with the reign of Snofru, who remained famous in the memory of the people. His foreign policy was quite active, and his military campaigns in Nubia and Libya had two objectives. One was the importation of thousands of prisoners to furnish a cheap labor force; the other was control of areas where minerals were extracted and the luxury products of Africa obtained. Three pyramids at two different sites are attributed to Snofru, one at Maidum and two at Dahshur.

The plateau of Giza, dominated by the pyramids of Khufu, Khephren, and Menkaure, is the most spectacular witness to the reigns of these three pharaohs of the Fourth Dynasty. These sovereigns, builders of what posterity has considered one of the Seven Wonders of the World, had the advantage of an absolute power over their people and of a faithful and devoted court. Their pyramids are surrounded by the cemeteries of private people, in which on both sides of the streets, one finds the names of the courtiers and dignitaries of their regimes carved on splendid mastabas. The sphinx, a majestic lion with the head of a king, entered into pharaonic iconography and came to recall the divine nature of the king, heir of the god Horus, who was believed in myth to have been the first king of the land.

Userkaf ascended the throne in 2510 B.C.E., opening the Fifth Dynasty, which is noted for the preeminence of the cult of the sun god. Henceforth the pharaohs would bear the title "son of Re," and they built sun temples at Abu Ghurab and at Abusir, near their pyramids. Following the foreign policies of their predecessors, they traded with Nubia, Sinai, and Syria-Palestine. Izezi and Wenis returned to Saqqara to be buried. The Pyramid Texts, a large collection of magical spells intended to allow the king, identified with the sun god, to encounter his peers in the afterlife, appeared on the walls of the royal tombs. The Fifth Dynasty was a prosperous one, and we note an appreciable increase in the number and power of its functionaries. Posthumous tradition attributed a collection of maxims to the vizier Ptahhotpe; their purpose was to induce obedience and respect for the established moral order.

At the end of the Fifth Dynasty (2460 B.C.E.), the Old Kingdom was at the height of its glory. But, the central government's gradual ceding of duties and powers to local authorities caused the rise of feudal systems that would escape the power of the kings of the Sixth Dynasty (2460–2200) and bring about their downfall. The great figures of that dynasty were Pepy I and Pepy II; Manetho attributed a reign of forty years to the former, and to the latter, one of ninety-five years! Political activities followed their course, and the conquest of Nubia was intensified, thanks to the colonization of el-Dakhla Oasis in the western desert. But intrigues and plots troubled life at court and endangered the kings themselves. Little by little, the administration was decentralized, and its legitimate powers seem to have eroded, to the profit of the local governors. These "nomarchs," as they are called, obtained privileges and immunities until, finally, they began to rule their own fiefs and were no longer accountable to the sovereign. The riches and opulence of the cemeteries of Upper and Middle Egypt serve as one of the best proofs of this ascent to power by provincial administrators. From Aswan to Deir el-Gabrawi, by way of Balat in el-Dakhla Oasis, the multiple chambers of vast mastabas are decorated with reliefs or paintings portraying the owner on his lands like a lord on his fief. We also know that the office of nomarch, previously appointed by the king, had become hereditary.

Among the major causes of the changes in the political, economic, and social orders in the Nile valley around 2200 B.C.E., we cannot overlook the climatic changes that occurred at that time. The wet phase came to an end, and the land was no longer watered by rainfall, which led to diminished agricultural output and the need for irrigation. At the same time, the increasing population had to concentrate itself in the valley, fleeing the steppes, which had become arid desert. It then devolved upon the nomarchs to create irrigation systems, with networks of canals, and this resulted in their effective control over the harvests in their region and their own ability to tax them on a regular basis.

THE FIRST INTERMEDIATE PERIOD

The designation that has become traditional for expressing the period stretching from the end of the Old Kingdom to the beginning of the Middle Kingdom, comprising the Seventh to the Eleventh Dynasties, is the First Intermediate Period. At its outset, it was characterized by a time of troubles, even revolution, whose violence was remembered as a horrible crisis by following generations. Riots led to the destruction of tombs, complete stoppage of work, and attacks on the offices of the administration. The gods were viewed with irony and skepticism; belief in the survival of the soul after death declined, and the prestige of the monarchy plummeted. The rich emigrated. Here and there, kinglets assumed the title King of Upper and Lower Egypt, heading the little states they carved out for themselves. The king list of Abydos, which enumerates the succession of the pharaohs, records twenty-five kings of the Eighth Dynasty alone, though it lasted only thirty years! In the delta, the situation was no brighter: invaders coming from the east, called "Asiatics" in the texts, assumed control of the region, and Bedouins formed alliances with them. In Middle Egypt, the site of Herakleopolis was the seat of a minicapital whose authority seems to have extended as far as Aswan. Starting about 2130 B.C.E., there was incessant strife between rival provinces, which sometimes lined up behind the prince of Thebes (modern Luxor) in Upper Egypt, and sometimes behind the prince of Herakleopolis in Middle Egypt. Victory was finally wrested in 2061 by Mentuhotpe II of Thebes, the fifth king of the Eleventh Dynasty.

THE MIDDLE KINGDOM: UNITY RESTORED

Thus began the Middle Kingdom (2060–1635 B.C.E.). The new dynasty, Theban in origin, soon pacified the land, placing men native to its own territory in charge of the provinces. In the thirty-ninth year of his reign, Mentuhotpe assumed the name "Sematawy," or "Uniter of the Two Lands," reflecting the reestablishment of pharaonic order throughout Egypt. This resumption of control over regional administration was accompanied by a great-works policy that filled the land with temples dedicated to the traditional gods: Osiris, Amun, Montu, Thoth. Military campaigns once again supplied Egypt with foreign products and laborers, and a string of fortresses was erected in the delta as a barrier against new invasions.

The Twelfth Dynasty (1991–1785 B.C.E.), with its Amenemhets and its Senwosrets, marked the apogee of the Middle Kingdom. The royal residence was moved: Itjtawy (the modern el-Lisht of the Faiyum), located at the junction of Upper and Lower Egypt, became the capital of the kingdom. Its intermediate geographic situation was advantageous for controlling all that went on in the provinces of both the north and the south. In the desert of el-Lisht were the pyramids of the pharaohs of the Twelfth Dynasty, more modest in size than those of their Old Kingdom predecessors but inspired by the same desire for the easiest possible access to the kingdom of Osiris, god of the hereafter.

The administration was entirely reformed. New offices necessitated a rapid and effective recruitment of scribes, and this urgent need for zealous functionaries led to the emergence of a middle class who could read and write and were prepared to serve their new employer faithfully. Their names are to be found on the innumerable funerary stelae discovered at Abydos near the sanctuary of Osiris, whose postmortem protection they proclaim.

Military campaigns subjugated Nubia as far south as the Second Cataract, where garrisons were stationed in immense fortresses, now engulfed by the waters of the High Dam at Aswan. In the north, Egyptian influence was felt as far away as Byblos, whose prince placed himself in a vassal relationship with his great neighbor. At Serabit el-Khadim, in the heart of Sinai, inscriptions commemorate nearly fifty expeditions that went there to quarry turquoise. The economy was prosperous: the Faiyum was developed, with new towns founded and the desert turned into arable land.

The overlong reigns of Senwosret III and Amenemhet III, each nearly a half-century, undoubtedly caused the decline and fall of this brilliant Twelfth Dynasty. The reign of a female pharaoh, Nefrusobk (1790–1785 B.C.E.), brought it to a close. The era after the Thirteenth Dynasty has been called by historians the "Second Intermediate Period" (1635–1580), even though it was not marked by revolution. It was, however, the end of the age of the pyramids; for thereafter, royal tombs no longer assumed the pyramid form so characteristic of the funerary customs of the most important pharaohs.

ABUNDANT BUT INCOMPLETE SOURCES

Egyptologists have several kinds of sources on which they can draw to bring the Egyptians from the time of the pyramids back to life in their daily activities. This documentation, which dates back five thousand years, can seem abundant at first glance; but specialized research daily runs into gaps in the record. One category of sources is contemporary texts written in hieroglyphs or hieratic, the latter a cursive form of hieroglyphs found on papyri or on potsherds (ostraca) used for rough drafts. A few papyrus documents, unfortunately fragmentary, yield precious information regarding the organization of work, life in the temples, details on how provisions were distributed, and so forth. The decipherment of the inscriptions carved by workers or their overseers in the mines and quarries, in Sinai or the Wadi Hammamat for example, makes a very useful contribution to our knowledge of expeditions. Archaeology and other field work are the other major category of sources. We are best informed about the world of Egypt by the tombs of private people and their scenes of daily life, annotated by columns of hieroglyphs, painted or carved on their rows of registers. Built for eternity, these tombs have withstood the vicissitudes of time better than private houses of unbaked brick or fragile papyri. For the Old Kingdom, up to six hundred decorated tombs can be counted from Giza to Aswan; their study has yielded a complete inventory of scenes of daily life. In preparing for their burial, ancient Egyptians wanted to be followed into the hereafter by concrete testimony of their lives in this world. To this end, they never failed to have the memorable events of their existence, the members of their families, their exercise of a profession, and a summary of their lives represented on the walls of their tombs.

With few exceptions, sources from the time of the pyramids are absent from the delta. The archaeological levels of this period either remain buried or have been entirely destroyed. But epigraphic and archaeological remains of prime importance for the period that concerns us are present in the valley, at the sites of Giza, Abu Rawash, Abusir, Saqqara, Dahshur, Maidum, el-Lisht, el-Lahun, Beni Hasan, Deir el-Gabrawi, el-Hawawish, Deir el-Bersha, Nag el-Deir, Abydos, Dendara, Luxor, el-Moalla, Edfu, and Aswan. In the 1960s, new light was shed on the relations between Egypt and Africa in the fourth and third millennia B.C.E. by work conducted in all haste before the Nubian sites settled in pharaonic times were swallowed up forever by the waters of the High Dam at Aswan. Outside the valley, in el-Dakhla Oasis, the recent excavations conducted by the French Institute of Oriental Archaeology at the site of Balat have permitted us to enlarge our field of investigation by gaining access to nonreligious sources whose existence had remained unsuspected; it has been possible to excavate several habitation sites. The remains of towns and villages, the ruins of Balat and el-Lahun, and the fortresses of Nubia permit us to form an idea of urbanism in unbaked brick in the pyramid age. Faced with these incomplete remains, the archaeologist can put together pieces of this ancient puzzle and reconstruct what everyday life was like on the banks of the Nile in the age of the pyramids.

2 PHARAOH'S SUBJECTS

Egypt was 630 miles in length, its provinces had marked regional characteristics, its delta was exposed to influences from the lands of Asia, and its economic system depended on permanent control of agricultural production. The country therefore was bound to create, at a very early date, powerful and effective administrative structures totally devoted to serving the pharaonic government.

Reigning over the country was Pharaoh, a personage endowed with a mythical nature grounded in dogma. In the opening lines of a Middle Kingdom text containing royal propaganda, we read, "His eyes probe every being. . . . He illumines the Two Lands (Upper and Lower Egypt) more than the sun disk. . . . He makes (things) green more than a great inundation. He fills the Two Lands with strength and life. Noses grow cold when he falls into a rage; when he is calmed, one breathes the air. He ensures the sustenance of those who follow him. . . . His enemy will be impoverished." In his essence, because he was the only possible intercessor between humans and their gods, Pharaoh was not a man like others. He was a man who played the role of a god and who exercised a divine function: that of Horus, who according to myth had been the first king of Egypt. The texts never fail to recall his semidivine nature, styling him "the son of the god," "the image of the god," "the beloved of the gods," "he who enjoys the favors of the gods." Beginning with Radjedef, the son and successor of Snofru, the kings proclaimed themselves "son of Re," thus placing themselves under the direct protection of the sun-god, the benefactor of humanity: "Re has placed the king in the land of the living forever and ever, to judge humankind and satisfy the gods, to do Good and destroy Evil." To legitimate this very special relationship he maintained with the gods, the pharaoh had at his disposal the "royal protocol," a five-fold titulary, developed during the Old Kingdom, which summed up his exceptional ancestry: in the course of his enthronement, Pharaoh received five "baptismal" names that called him, in succession, the heir of Horus and of Nekhbet and Wadjit (the tutelary goddesses of Upper and Lower Egypt), a falcon of gold (the flesh of the gods), king of Upper and Lower Egypt, and, as we have seen, the son of Re. As for the bas-reliefs in temples and chapels, they show the sovereign welcomed into the world of the gods as one of their own: he speaks to deities as equal to equal and receives from them the qualities that make him a unique being. It was under their protection that the sovereign would exercise his function, whose goal was, essentially, to implement all the measures necessary to maintain *Maat*. On this fundamental notion, which simultaneously embraced social peace, justice, truth, order, trust, and all the imaginable harmonious forces that made the world inhabitable, depended the equilibrium of the state, and even of the cosmos. The death of a king was a disaster befalling the land; only the accession of his successor would reestablish the order willed by the gods and desired by humankind. At his death, the king flew off to the paradise of the gods. The fictitious "Story of Sinuhe" recounts that at the death of Amenemhet I "in year 30, the third month of the season *akhet*, the seventh day, . . . the king of Upper and Lower Egypt Sehetepibre flew off to the sky and united with the sun disk, while his divine limbs joined those of his Creator. The royal Residence was plunged into silence, hearts were aggrieved, the great double gate of the Palace remained closed, the courtiers were bent down, their heads on their knees, and the people uttered cries of lamentation."

Pharaoh's clothing, attributes, and emblems also connected him to the divine realm. He wore not the ordinary loincloth of people here below, but rather the pleated *shendjyt*-apron with its triangular frontpiece. From his belt hung a bull's tail, a reminder that his power equaled that of the animal. Like the gods, his chin was adorned with a false beard, which could be straight or curved. An essential element, a crown, completed the costume; Pharaoh never went bareheaded. Whichever crown he wore was chosen for the occasion and conferred on him a specific power suited to the event. The Double Crown was a combination of the Red and White Crowns, symbols of Lower and Upper Egypt. Joined together on the king's head, they designated his exercise of power over the two constitutive parts of his realm. Most often, his headdress was the *nemes*, a sort of striped kerchief whose two sidepieces hung down over his chest. Sphinxes, which are leonine images of the kings, all wear the *nemes*. Above his brow, the *nemes* was adorned with a uraeus, a female cobra, rearing up like a protective shield, whose fiery breath annihilated all his enemies. In his hands, the king held insignia of his prestige: a long, curved staff, recalling that of a shepherd leading a flock, and a lash, which also served as a fly whisk.

ON THE DIFFICULTY OF BEING KING

But Pharaoh was also a man, subject to illness and plain old age. To renew the strength and vigor of the sovereign, a jubilee ritual was celebrated, whose origins dated back to the earliest years of the historical era. In theory at least, this *sed*-festival was celebrated after thirty years of rule, and then every three or four years; its purpose was the regeneration of the king's physical strength and magical powers. After the ritual burial of a statue of the aged king, the "rejuvenated" king visited various sanctuaries throughout the land. There, a retinue of priests and dignitaries would view the spectacle of the king engaging in athletic exercises, such as footracing and archery, manifestations of his recovered youth.

Most sources available to Egyptologists belong to the official literature issued by palace offices in the service of royal ideology. Thus it is difficult to discern the personalities and shortcomings of the pharaohs hidden behind the phraseology of this propaganda. Nevertheless, a few royal figures from the time of the pyramids do emerge to provide us with a nuanced vision of these personages. Snofru (2625–2605 B.C.E.) appears in posthumous tradition as a generous and beneficent king, whereas his son Khufu (2605–2580) had the reputation of having been a bloody and despotic pharaoh who demanded, for example, that his entourage cut off a man's head to see whether his magician would succeed in reattaching it. The statue head of Radjedef (2580–2570), now in the Louvre, reveals a man filled with concentration and gentleness; we can easily believe he cared about human suffering. But the numerous portraits of the aged Senwosret III (1878–1842) are especially striking because of the seriousness and sadness they express (Figure 2). Abandoning the representation of himself with the features of an eternally young and dynamic man, as official convention would have had it, Senwosret III displays a face marked by time and weariness, stamped with humanity and concern for others.

A few texts written by kings who experienced grave ordeals in the course of their reigns also shed precious light on Pharaoh's circumstances. The "Instruction for Merykare," a king of the Tenth Dynasty, and the "Instruction of Amenemhet I" for his son Senwosret I (c. 1965 B.C.E.) are personal tes-

FIGURE 2.
Statue head of Senwosret III. Louvre E12362. © Chuzeville. Photo courtesy of The Louvre.

timonies of the human difficulties these pharaohs encountered during their reigns; each unburdens himself to his successor in a sort of testament both lucid and disillusioned. Amenemhet I escaped an assassination plot concocted by his courtiers and felt betrayed by his own people. Just like the father of Merykare, he preaches distrust yet recommends striving to make oneself loved, being merciful, and mistreating no one.

The remains of royal palaces of the age, to the extent they exist, are in such a poor state of preservation it is difficult to reconstruct the physical setting of the pharoah's life. But the mortuary furniture of Queen Hetepheres, Khufu's mother, which was discovered intact in 1925, reveals an art of palace living characterized by great sophistication and a sense of refined comfort (Figure 3). A large dais of gold-plated wood, which could be disassembled, sheltered the royal family during open-air ceremonies, and an ebony litter carried by bearers permitted them to move about without setting foot on the ground. The rest of the furnishings — a bed, arm-

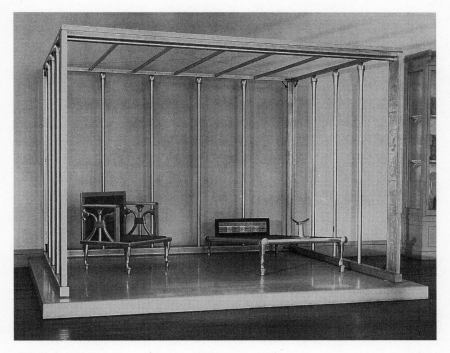

FIGURE 3.

Replica of some of the mortuary furniture of Queen Hetepheres. Left: chair (MFA 38.957); right: bed (MFA 29.1858). Surrounding them: bed canopy (MFA 38.873). Departmental Appropriation, May 1938. Courtesy, Museum of Fine Arts, Boston.

chairs, chairs, and wares — are of very high quality craftsmanship and distinguished by sobriety and refinement.

THE VIZIER, PHARAOH'S PRIME MINISTER

As holder of all the powers, the pharaoh had more to do than he could handle. In theory, he was the only landowner in the country, the only priest, the only judge, and the only warrior. To accomplish all his tasks, he surrounded himself with ministers and officials who worked under the supervision of the vizier, the veritable prime minister of the pharaonic government. In the Old Kingdom, all key posts in the administration were entrusted to high officials chosen from the royal family, which resided in Memphis, capital of the land and seat of the central government. At their deaths, beautiful carved and painted mastabas were constructed for them in the cemeteries of Giza and Saqqara, near the pyramids of their sovereigns. Their titularies, which can be read on the doorjambs of their tombs, inform us of their degree of kinship with the royal person and of the ministerial positions they occupied. The abundance of titles and functions reveals an administration already highly organized into a hierarchy of bureaus, departments, and subdepartments.

Over centuries, there were considerable changes in the responsibilities of the vizier and how he was recruited, but a text known as the "Installation of the Vizier" gives a good idea of the role of this important personage in the first half of the second millennium. At his installation ceremony, the vizier heard a speech by the king, who asked him above all to exercise justice and to resolve the difficulties that happen at every turn: "Assume the office of vizier, attend to everything that is done in its name; for it is the support of the whole land. Indeed, the vizierate is not sweet; it is bitter as bile." The responsibilities were so great, moreover, that the office had sometimes to be allotted to two or three men, each vizier to be in charge of one administrative section of the country or one particular function. For the vizier had authority over all domains: justice, agriculture, irrigation, police, public order, and allocation of lands, as well as supervision of state grain supplies, taxes, finances, construction projects, and expeditions to mines and quarries.

The geographic and topographic characteristics of Egypt greatly complicated its administration. How, indeed, was it possible to exercise effective control over provinces separated from the capital by several days of navigation or foot travel? The solution was to decentralize some of the authority among officials transferred to the provinces or, better still, among local notables. In exchange for their services, the king accorded them considerable privileges and concessions, a process that accelerated under the Sixth Dynasty. Thus were established the "nomes," provinces dividing the territory of Egypt into so many administrative entities under the direction of "nomarchs." The temptation to set themselves up as independent potentates was strong, and they were not all equally loyal to the central authority, particularly as the Memphite government grew weaker. At the end of the Sixth Dynasty (c. 2200 B.C.E.), Qar was appointed nomarch at Edfu, nearly five hundred miles south of the capital; he resisted the wave of autonomy and recalled, without modesty, his loyalty to Pharaoh Merenre: "The Majesty of Merenre had me sail upstream to the nome of Edfu as sole companion, nomarch, overseer of Upper Egyptian barley and overseer of prophets, because I was capable and appreciated in the esteem of His Majesty. I came to be accorded the office of lord of every leader of all Upper Egypt. . . . I acted so that the bulls of this nome were more numerous than the bulls that were in the stables of all Upper Egypt. This is indeed not something I found accomplished by my predecessor . . . because I was vigilant and effectiveness prevailed when I managed affairs for the Residence. . . . I gave bread to the hungry and clothing to the one who went naked in this nome. . . . It was I who buried every man in this nome who had no heir, with linen drawn from my own property. I subjected all foreign countries to the Residence, so effective was my vigilance in this regard, and I was rewarded for that by my lord." Perhaps this self-satisfaction was not exaggerated; for this nomarch displayed such charisma in his province that he was one of the few human beings to be deified and made the object, after his death, of a cult of his own.

The most important ministry was that of the Treasury, on which the economy of the land depended. Placed under the direct control of the vizier, it was divided into two offices: the "White Treasury" was in charge of the finances of Upper Egypt and worked in parallel with the "Red Treasury," which dealt with the affairs of Lower Egypt. Their role was fiscal and budgetary: tax collection, and the redistribution of raw materials and revenues according to the economic needs of the state, including construction works. The "overseer of the two granaries" and his numerous assistants busied themselves alongside the representatives of the Treasury; their role was to keep records of the commodities stockpiled in the royal storehouses as a result of the annual taxes.

THE ADMINISTRATIVE REFORMS
OF THE MIDDLE KINGDOM

After the First Intermediate Period (2200–2060 B.C.E.), which saw a collapse of central power and the dismantling of the political structures of the Old Kingdom, the pharaohs of the Twelfth Dynasty (1991–1785) and their viziers designed the administration differently. Rather than depend on important regional families, they felt that the loyalty of the administrative personnel could be more reliably secured by recruiting their ranks from the middle class. Fearing lest they see the country fall back into anarchy and the granaries deprived of wheat, lower-middle-class Egyptians had everything to gain by entering the administration, which was hiring in great numbers in the hope of restoring central authority. Schools were opened, scribes were trained, and jobs were allocated throughout the public sector; and thus, within two generations, a class of devoted civil servants was created. The capital was moved to el-Lisht, in Middle Egypt, which accommodated the new government departments.

The city teemed with scribes; for there was so much to record, copy, and file away. Pleased with their recent rise in social status, functionaries would attempt to bring their relatives into their "socioprofessional" field. Thus, in a family dedicated to maintaining order, we note that a father who was a gendarme had a son who was a policeman, a brother who was a guard, and a nephew who was an officer of the law. Hope of promotion or reward could prompt some men to display extreme zealousness in the performance of their duties. On his funerary stelae, Dedusobk, a police commissioner, boasts that he was one "who knew how to make the dissembler talk, who knew a man at his speech, who could make a body reveal what it had hidden, who caused the heart to spit up what it had swallowed . . . who satisfied the king by seeking and punishing the troublemaker, who prepared the trial with which he had fully acquainted himself, one whose granaries the king filled abundantly."

Nevertheless, a certain prudence was recommended to this new class of parvenus. As early as their school days, they were advised, "Do not corrupt magistrates, and do not incite a just man to rebellion. Do not have more regard for the well-dressed; do not despise the one dressed in rags. Do not accept the gifts of a powerful man, and do not persecute a weak one." Humility and patience were the secret to an honorable career; for there was an oppressive hierarchy in the administrative offices, and promotion was not automatic. The manuals of conduct insist so often on the dangers of corruption that we can only conclude it was rampant. In the mind of the governed, official dishonesty was resented as an offense against the order established by Maat, and it became the subject of certain of the most popular works of literature. Thus the "Story of the Eloquent Peasant" portrays a man from the countryside who was robbed of his goods by a highwayman and who came to the city to plead his case before a high judicial official. Endless discussions ensued. Amused by the plaintiff's speeches, the man of law remained indifferent, which led to the comparison of an unjust official to "a city without a mayor, a group without a leader, a boat without a captain . . . a policeman who has become a thief, a mayor who takes bribes," whereas an honest official was "a father to the orphan, a husband to the widow, a brother to the divorced woman, a nurse to the motherless."

FOREIGN POLICY

Foreign affairs, war, and territorial conquest belonged to the domain reserved for Pharaoh. To triumph over an enemy was another way to enforce Maat. This image of the pharaoh as warrior and protector is well expressed in a hymn to Senwosret III (1878–1842 B.C.E.): "Hail to you . . . [who subdues] foreign lands by the force of his hands, who slays barbarians without the blow of a club, who shoots arrows without drawing the bowstring. The mere terror the king inspires smites the Nubians in their land; the mere fear he inspires slays the Asiatics. . . . He is a youth, unique and divine, [who fights] for his frontiers, who does not let his subjects know weariness, who allows people to sleep until daylight."

In the field, Pharaoh surrounded himself with a council of astute generals, as well as officers, professional soldiers, and fighting men. In the time of the pyramids, the professional army consisted of regiments too small to be compared with those it would have beginning with the New Kingdom, when kings named Amenophis and Ramesses would battle relentlessly with their neighbors. Egyptians were by nature peaceful, more inclined to cultivate their fields or fish in the marshes than to bear arms. There is no word in the Egyptian vocabulary corresponding to our word *war*; at the very most, we find terms designating combat or battle. Fortunately, the deserts and the Mediterranean were natural bulwarks against potential enemies, but they did not entirely keep them out. Bedouins from Asia, the "Sanddwellers," could make their appearance by way of Sinai and the delta, or Nubians from Africa through the corridor of the Nile; from the dawn of history, these appear to have been the traditional enemies of the country. In defeat, they would in their turn be enrolled in the fighting army and form elite troops much sought after to fight alongside the Egyptians.

A soldier can be recognized by the "uniform" accorded him in the bas-reliefs and paintings: most often, he went naked, with a penis sheath attached to his waist and a feather stuck in his hair. On the march, he wore a short loincloth and carried his shield and weapons in his hands as he stepped along. In hand-to-hand combat, the soldier used a club, an axe, and a knife made of sharp flint. The weapons most commonly used to attack an enemy from a distance were the bow and arrow, and sometimes the sling-shot and the boomerang. The only defensive weapon known was the shield, made of wood covered with leather.

A few battle scenes from the Old Kingdom yield precious details of fighting tactics. For the most part, their action takes place in Palestine, around a fortress under attack by the Egyptians. In the Sixth Dynasty tomb of Kaemhezet at Saqqara (c. 2250 B.C.E.), soldiers are seen attacking a fortified camp by sapping and with blows of the axe; inside, men, women, children, and cattle are holed up. A group of Egyptians scales the wall with the help of a ladder that they move by pushing it along on wheels. In the distance, hand-to-hand combat ensues, while a shepherd, perceiving that his camp has lost the day, tries to make his animals flee. At Dishasha in Middle Egypt, a relief in the Fifth Dynasty tomb of Inti (c. 2480) is even more vivid, because of the hieroglyphic legends that accompany it. Soldiers group together at the foot of the fortress, while archers make ready. Hand-to-hand combat has already ensued between Egyptians armed with axes and their enemies, who are armed with maces but have already been wounded by arrows shot from a distance. Then the assault takes place, both above and below: some men climb a ladder to penetrate the fortress, while others dig a tunnel under the ramparts. Within the high walls, there is desolation. One man tries to silence the cries in order to hear the thuds of the battering ram shaking the walls, but his commandant is at his wit's end: he is tearing his hair out, deaf to the words of the woman at his feet. Women are tending to the wounded or are about to expose some cowards who are hiding; an old man snatches a child from his mother, hoping to find shelter for him. The combat is unequal, and soon a file of prisoners, each tied to the one behind him, is escorted by an Egyptian soldier who carries a little girl on his shoulders, like so much booty.

These warlike incursions into Palestine were sporadic, and their sole intent was to crush the spirit of the Asiatics and thus secure a buffer zone alongside the isthmus of Suez. Weni, a favorite of King Pepy I (c. 2300 B.C.E.), was sent by the king to repel a raid by nomads. His long autobiographical inscription describes his exploits as a general with enthusiasm and exaltation. After noting all the recruits he had to levy, including Nubian mercenaries, he continues: "It was I who furnished them (the governors of the regions in question) with the plan, . . . because of the precision of my organization, so that no one offended against one of his fellows, so that no one stole bread or sandals from those who were along the way, so that no one stole a garment in any town, so that no one took any goat from anyone." Curiously, Weni gives no technical details of the battle for which he had so well prepared; rather, he proceeds immediately to state the results: "This army returned in peace, having razed the land of the 'Sand-dwellers' to the ground. This army returned in peace, having ravaged the land of the

'Sand-dwellers.' This army returned in peace, having toppled its fortified towns. This army returned in peace, having cut down its fig trees and vineyards. This army returned in peace, having set fire to all its men. This army returned in peace, having killed a great number of its troops. This army returned in peace, having taken a great number of prisoners."

General Weni was sent on punitive expeditions against the "Sand-dwellers" on five occasions and then on a mission to Nubia, with the sole aim of bringing back red granite for the construction of the king's pyramid. In Phoenicia, peaceful commercial relations were being established with Byblos: it was from there that the Egyptian state imported fir and cedar in quantity for boat building and for the coffins intended for the ruling class.

EGYPT AND AFRICA

In the Old Kingdom, trade was the reason for military campaigns in Africa. Troops ready to contend with peoples hostile to the land of Pharaoh were periodically sent into Lower Nubia to clear the route to the regions producing the commodities and materials of which the Egyptians were so fond. Harkhuf, an Upper Egyptian administrator around 2250 B.C.E., led three expeditions into the heart of Africa, which he describes on the door-jambs of his tomb at Aswan: "I came back to Egypt with three hundred donkeys laden with incense, ebony, *hekenu*-oil, *sat*-grain, panther skins, elephant tusks, and every beautiful, valuable thing." Harkhuf did not tell everything in this inscription; for elsewhere he reproduced a letter his king had dispatched to him: "You said . . . that you have brought back every excellent and beautiful product. . . . You said . . . that you have brought back a pygmy from the land of the horizon-dwellers for the dances of the gods. . . . Come down to court immediately, and bring this pygmy with you. . . . My Majesty desires to see this pygmy more than all the wonders of the land of Punt." On these expeditions, the Egyptians took advantage of the opportunity to recruit Nubian troops, whose battalions formed a special corps of archers within the army.

A PROFESSIONAL ARMY

After the First Intermediate Period (2200–2060 B.C.E.), which had seen power-hungry princes killing one another and Egyptians attacking their own brothers, it seemed necessary to maintain a large-scale professional army, as much to maintain order at home as to conquer other territories.

Again, it was from the middle class that the rulers of the Twelfth Dynasty recruited their new military cadres. Militias based in the towns and villages can be discerned, as well as warriors and escorts who served both in combat and as armed battalions whose job was to accompany expeditions to the mines and quarries.

The sovereigns of the Twelfth Dynasty (1991–1785 B.C.E.) first took up arms against Nubia, conducting a systematic colonialist policy by which they sought to "enlarge their frontiers" through every possible means. We thus witness the colonization and Egyptianization of Lower Nubia as far as the Second Cataract, as evidenced by the text of a border stela, inscribed under Senwosret III (1878–1842) and erected at Semna, more than three hundred miles south of Aswan: "Southern frontier, made in year 8 under the Majesty of the King of Upper and Lower Egypt . . . , may he live forever and ever, to prevent any Nubian from crossing it . . . by boat or with any Nubian herds, unless this Nubian comes to trade at Buhen, or with a message or something else that augurs good, but for all that, without allowing any Nubian boat ever to pass by Semna traveling north." Semna and Buhen are the names of two of the seven fortresses built on the cliffs of the river, upstream from the swift rapids of the Second Cataract. This string of river fortresses is the earliest known example of military architecture organized into a network defending several sites. Engulfed today by the lake created by the High Dam at Aswan, the Nubian fortresses have yielded precious details of the life that unfolded within their high walls, thanks to several campaigns of excavation hastily conducted by teams of archaeologists before they were finally chased off by the rising waters. Housing areas, administrative buildings, sanctuaries, and barracks were laid out side by side, behind a double wall that had semicircular bastions and angled towers, with curtain walls between them. The path round the battlements formed almost a complete square. All the fortresses were judiciously adapted to the topography of their locales, which were more or less steep; but they were all huge: the surface area of the site of Buhen has been estimated at more than 110,000 square miles. All the architectural elements of military defense employed in the fortifications of medieval Europe were already known in Egyptian Nubia at the beginning of the second millennium B.C.E.

LIFE IN THE COLONIES

The Egyptians stationed in Nubia were principally career soldiers, along with some scribes serving as administrators. The remainder all bore titles designating patrol, surveillance, and border-police functions. The documentation relating to these sites often consists of dispatches sent from one fortress to another, recounting inspection missions: "The patrol that left to patrol in the desert, on the righthand side of the fortress Khesef-Medjayu (the ancient name of Serra), has returned, making the following report: 'We found the trail of 32 men and 3 donkeys.'" Other documents testify to the boredom of the Egyptians living there and to their desire for instructions and news from the capital. The colonists transferred to these far-off places brought along their families and, in the end, created a unique life style, influenced by local customs. This aspect is especially striking in their artistic production: an Egyptian statue made in the Nubian workshops of the Middle Kingdom displays thick features, disproportionate limbs, and an overall clumsiness that makes us doubt whether its sculptor ever left his fortress.

Egypt of the Middle Kingdom did not have this sort of expansionist aim in Asia. Moreover, the nomadic life style of the Bedouins and the landscape of Palestine and the Lebanon were troubling to the Egyptian world. Accustomed to their river and their deserts, the Nile dwellers were hardly attracted by this land of forested mountains or by the Mediterranean coast, where rain and even snow fell regularly. In a passage from the "Instruction for King Merykare," we read: "The poor Asiatic, difficult is the place where he is. It is attacked by water and inaccessible because of the many trees; the roads are difficult because of the mountains. He cannot dwell in a fixed place; he must be ever on the move." Thus the sole object of the military operations conducted in Asia by the pharaohs of the Twelfth Dynasty was to control the movements of the Bedouins and keep clear the routes leading to the rare products of the regions of Palestine, Syria, and the Lebanon. Moreover, there are no archaeological remains serving as evidence of Egyptian installations like those found in Lower Nubia. To be sure, there are some royal or private inscriptions describing victorious warlike operations, like that of general Nesmontu: "I defeated the Asiatics who dwell on the sand; I destroyed their strongholds, approaching them stealthily. I came, and I traveled all their paths." But there is good cause to think this statement entails some boasting.

The tomb of the nomarch Khnumhotpe at Beni Hasan, from the reign of Senwosret II (1895–1878 B.C.E.), shows a caravan of Palestinian traders, who undoubtedly came from Moab, east of the Red Sea, bringing their exotic wares. Khnumhotpe was in charge of controlling the eastern frontier of Egypt, and he was thus in a good position to negotiate with Bedouin tribes for the importation of cosmetics and of the arms made in their homeland: javelins, lances, arrows, and bows. The physical appearance of the Palestinians represented in the tomb characterizes them immediately as foreigners. The men have curly beards and frizzy hair; their loincloths are dyed and striped; and their feet are shod in lattice-work sandals. As for their women, they have light eyes and wear multicolored dresses and leather ankle boots.

During the Thirteenth Dynasty (c. 1750 B.C.E.), foreign groups from Asia, called "Hyksos," settled in the delta and established trading centers there. The two communities, Egyptian and Syro-Palestinian, coexisted peacefully, as witnessed by the recent excavations conducted at Tell el-Daba in the eastern delta. Economic interests, sealed by matrimonial alliances, enabled the two cultures to live side by side without discord. But at the end of the Middle Kingdom, at the time of the last pyramids, when the central power again collapsed, threat followed by invasion would come from Asia.

In the middle of the second millennium, the geopolitical facts of the Near East changed totally. The pharaonic state would have to adapt, obliging the Egyptian people to emerge from their splendid isolation and acquire an awareness of neighboring peoples. From then on, they would often have to take up arms and wage war beyond their frontiers.

3 PUBLIC WORKS

Architect of creation in his kingdom, Pharaoh was an indefatigable builder, expending boundless energy and colossal resources on the constructions required by the cults of the gods, the funerary customs, and the life of the people. To help him in his monumental program, he counted on the assistance of his vizier. The latter bore the title "overseer of all the works of the king," which indicated his role in organizing and supervising the royal workshops and the sites of Pharaoh's great constructions.

THE ROYAL PYRAMID, FOREMOST CONSTRUCTION SITE OF THE STATE

The most important project of the vizier's career was, as one might expect, the building of the royal pyramid. Its work force was levied from the peasant population, according to a system of obligatory corvée labor. This was a sort of conscription that made the peasants, Pharaoh's subjects, liable to requisition at any time for major public projects: the construction of roads, irrigation canals, the building of monuments, or expeditions to the mines and quarries. Yet we cannot speak of slavery in pharaonic Egypt, either for the purpose of pyramid building or for any other major project. The construction of the royal tombs, gigantic though they were, was presented, and in general perceived, as a great "national" cause from which one could not shirk, any more than from war or the development of new agricultural lands. And so, just as Pharaoh wished, his subjects played their role, eager to obey royal orders and make their contribution to the construction of the world.

This corvée system survived long after the pharaonic period; not until the year 1889 of our own era was it finally abolished. Periodically, the sovereign had his administrative offices issue decrees of exemption intended to relieve some part of the work force from this obligation. Considerable privileges were thus granted, most often directed at the priests and personnel of the royal funerary complexes who worked in the "pyramid cities." Pepy I (c. 2300 B.C.E.) proclaimed, "My Majesty has commanded the perpetual exemption of these two pyramid cities from any work for the royal palace, from any obligatory work for a place of the Residence, as well as such corvée as is demanded of anyone." In the Middle Kingdom, these privileges were extended to the new middle class, which was composed principally of scribes dedicated to the restoration of a sound administration. A sentiment of revolt then appeared among the working people harassed by these incessant requisitions, causing some of those subject to corvée to take flight. This phenomenon, which historians call "anachoresis," grew more widespread in Egypt in the course of the centuries. It must have assumed serious proportions in the Roman period; for contemporary authors describe villages housing only old men, women, and children. The situation was not as dramatic in the Middle Kingdom, but certain administrative documents of that period routinely list fugitives side by side with conscripts. Desertion was punished by a life sentence of forced labor: "[Order] issued by the Great [Prison], in year 31, third month of summer, fifth day: that he be condemned, with his family, to work for life on the state-owned lands, [according to] the decision of the court of justice." The lives of these men were then placed in the hands of officials whose job it was to exploit them for the benefit of the state. Deprived of their liberty, these people were moved from estate to estate, and they could even be given to others or conveyed by inheritance. In the testament of a landowner who supervised a goodly number of these captured runaways, we read: "My fifteen people and the prisoners in my house are to be given to my wife Senebtisy, in addition to the sixty I gave her the first time. . . . I transmit this title deed to my wife . . . and she in her turn will be able to make it over to the one she wishes of the children she has given me. . . . I also make over to her the four Asiatics my father made over to me." Prisoners of war — Asiatics and Nubians — were an important supplement to the labor force. Some raids conducted in neighboring lands, particularly against the Bedouins of Asia, were intended to bring back men on the cheap.

MINES AND QUARRIES

The expeditions to the mines and quarries under the orders of Pharaoh and the vizier were as impressive as the ensuing construction works. The conscripts often had to travel to a far-off, inhospitable desert in search of the treasures to be found there: stone for construction, ores, and other minerals. Supervision of the operations was entrusted to the "royal chancellor of the two fleets" or the "overseer of troops." Other officials bore important titles of the national navy: we find captains and ship's officers, as though the expedition troops had been assimilated to a naval battalion, with a port crew and a starboard crew, the rowers having been replaced by the quarrymen. The basic unit was one hundred men, divided into groups of ten. Each unit had a name: "the great," "the pure," "the august," "the satisfied." We also note a considerable administrative staff of scribes, interpreters, and overseers of the treasury. Expeditions never set off without the invaluable assistance of the *nuu*, experts in the trails whom we also find in scenes of hunting desert game and who are encountered here prospecting the mines and quarries in search of new veins. They took advantage of the occasion to monitor the movements of nomads and to give chase to fugitives, those very men who were attempting to escape the corvée.

Most of the mines and quarries were located in the eastern desert, between the Nile and the Red Sea, or in the Sinai Peninsula. There, the quarrymen and their overseers carved hundreds of graffiti and more carefully executed inscriptions on the rock walls (Figure 4), which yield valuable information on the composition, date, and organization of expeditions. Tools were few: to fashion their blocks, the stonecutters employed picks of hard, heavy basalt, which they fitted into wooden tongs or held in their bare hands. On gemstones, they used copper chisels, which they hit with basalt hammers or wooden mallets. On soft stone, they made use of a copper saw, whose teeth were covered with sand during the cutting process. The surface was leveled by pounding it lightly with the help of a ball of dolerite and then steadily rubbing it with an abrasive powder of ground quartzite.

The quarries of Hatnub, a three-hour trek to the southeast of the region of el-Amarna, yielded calcite, a stone similar to alabaster. It was difficult to work but still much sought after for carving statues, vases, offering tables, and sometimes even small chapels. With its transparency and its veins of marbled color ranging from nearly pure black to light brown, it was a material destined for delicate objects, such as the funerary vessels of the royal

FIGURE 4.
Rock inscriptions at Wadi Hammamat. Photo by Guillemette Andreu.

tombs. The quarries of Hatnub were controlled by the governors of the province of Hermopolis, who exploited them while jealously guarding their monopoly. Extraordinary exploits took place during the lifetime of one of them, Djehutihotpe (c. 1850 B.C.E.), and he had them represented in his tomb at Deir el-Bersha. Image and text vividly depict the extraction of a colossal statue, over twenty feet in height and weighing more than seventy tons, and its transport over a nine-mile route (Figure 5). Its extraction took place underground; the workers had to pass through a long tunnel whose ceiling threatened to collapse. The stone was evidently sculpted on the spot, in the open air, or at least was roughly hewed. It then had to be attached to a sledge with ropes that girdled it in all directions. Care was taken to put pieces of cloth at the corners and friction points, to prevent the ropes from causing the stone to splinter. The ropes of the sledge bearing the statue were pulled by 172 men, divided into four rows. To facilitate their effort, one man constantly poured water in front of the sledge, thus helping it to move along on ground transformed into clayey mud. This representation confirms the assumptions of archaeologists regarding the overland transport of blocks of stone for construction or sculpting. It was not the wheel, but

FIGURE 5.

Transport of the colossal statue of Djehutihotpe; only some of the 172 men
depicted dragging the statue are represented here. From his tomb at Deir el-
Bersha. After C. R. Lepsius, Denkmaeler aus Aegypten und Aethiopien
(Berlin: Nicolai, 1849–56), Part 2, Plate 134.

rather the sledge, that served to transport these heavy loads; it rested on
logs that were moved as the device progressed along a wetted, slippery path.
Perched on the knees of the colossal statue of the governor, the overseer
gave his orders, ably directing the operations. The statue was intended for
Djehutihotpe himself; in the accompanying legend, he expresses his pride
in having brought this impossible transport task to a successful conclusion:
"Transport of a statue of thirteen cubits (just over twenty-two feet), of stone
of Hatnub. Behold, the route by which it came was very difficult, more than
all the rest. Behold, the hauling of this load [. . .] was very painful for the
heart of the men, because of the rough, stony ground composed of hard
rock. I had young men come, the relief team of the recruits, to construct a

road for the statue, as well as teams of quarrymen, administrators, and specialists. The strong people said, 'We can do it,' and my heart rejoiced. The city assembled and let out cries of joy. The spectacle was more beautiful than anything. The old man . . . leaned on the young one; strong and weak helped together, and their courage grew. Their arms became strong, and a single one among them displayed the strength of a thousand men. Behold, this statue, which came from the great mountain in a single block, was more valuable than all the rest. . . . I arrived in this city, and the people gathered in a single praise." Evidently this was a popular and entertaining spectacle with positive repercussions on the political career of the governor.

WADI HAMMAMAT

A hundred miles from Koptos in Upper Egypt, point of departure for caravan routes and the exploration of the eastern quarries, the schistose valley of the Wadi Hammamat sparkles in the desert sun. On both sides of the route, one sees traces of an immense, open-air quarry that was the source of a beautiful, hard, dark stone, sometimes amber green and sometimes very dark gray. From the Old Kingdom on, royal and divine sarcophagi and statues were made of this stone. In year 38 of Senwosret I (c. 1935 B.C.E.), the royal herald Ameny conducted a gigantic expedition, comprising more than 17,000 men, to the Wadi Hammamat. Their mission was to bring back to the royal workshops the raw material for 60 sphinxes and 150 statues. Each statue was dragged by a group of 1,500, 1,000, or 500 men, according to its weight. Ameny's inscription draws up a list of his officials, administrative staff, specialized workers, and the rank and file, cataloged according to their hierarchical status and social class. Opposite their names are noted their allotted daily food rations. We thus see that Ameny, the overseer of the expedition, received on average one hundred times more bread and fifty times more beer than the unhappy conscript laborer. But the gods watched over the expeditions to the Wadi Hammamat and manifested themselves through the intervention of miraculous events. One day, a gazelle gave birth on a beautiful block of stone that the workers had not spotted. It was a sign from the god: the rock would become the lid of the sarcophagus ordered by the reigning monarch. A few days later, a second wonder occurred at the same site. A miraculous rainfall that "showed the power of the god to the men" drew attention to a natural well until then undiscovered. The inscription relating these events gives thanks to Min, the "august god, lord of the deserts" and patron of its mines and trails. Close to the schist quarries of the Wadi Hammamat were some gold mines worked intermittently in the time of the pyramids. The veins of gold-bearing quartz were located by the *sementiu*, specialists in prospecting easily recognized by the sack they carried on the shoulder, used in gathering their mineral samples. The laborers then came and crushed the blocks to extract the particles of precious metal. Next, women washed the powder thus obtained and sifted the flakes. Crushing and washing areas have been discovered near watering holes, but for lack of inscriptions, they cannot be dated.

WADI EL-HUDI AND GEBEL ZEIT

Further south in the eastern desert, twenty-two miles south-east of As-wan, the Wadi el-Hudi is home to quartz, gold, carnelian, and amethyst. In the Middle Kingdom, the same important personages, expedition leaders who had become experts in supervising troops in these desert areas, are often found in the Wadi Hammamat, the Wadi el-Hudi, and even in Sinai. The workers no longer regularly came from Koptos; of the 1,500 men who made up a large-scale expedition, 100 were from Kom Ombo and 200 from Elephantine, near Aswan.

Situated on the shore of the Red Sea, the mountainous massif of Gebel Zeit harbors a small mining site composed of galleries, housing, and a sanc-tuary, which were constructed by the teams who went there to extract ga-lena, the lead sulfide from which kohl was made. Archaeological investiga-tions in this area have made it possible to reconstruct the life of these miners in the Middle Kingdom. Having departed from Koptos, the men on expe-dition to Gebel Zeit arrived at the site, few in number and to stay but a few weeks. They had to bring their means of subsistence from home: lentils, favas and other beans, wheat, and barley have been found in their bags. The camp was located on an elevation, enabling them to keep watch over the approaches to the site, look at the sea, and control visitors. Once set up, they began to prospect the ground in order to detect the veins of galena, which they could follow to reach the galleries or simple shafts. Some galler-ies had branches descending nearly a hundred feet below ground level. The spot where the vein was penetrated could be separated from the open air by more than 325 feet, which made the mining process especially slow and difficult. The tools were picks and hard stone hammers, which were made near the crushing areas. Not far from the camp, the diggers cleared a cir-cular enclosure, which served as a minimal cult site (Figure 6). On each new

FIGURE 6.
The cult site at Gebel Zeit. Photo by Guillemette Andreu.

expedition, the miners climbed back over the walls, which collapsed from one year to the next, and removed the cultic equipment and votive objects from the cache where they had hidden them when they departed at the end of the previous season. To make them feel secure, they brought a new lot of stelae, very small ones and thus easily carried in their bags, along with their food.

The most astonishing archaeological material from Gebel Zeit is a series of small baked-clay figurines found in the sanctuary (Figure 7). These "dolls" personified slender, nude women whose thin faces were topped by very elaborate hair made of linen and sometimes adorned with beads. The bodies of some were dotted with circular incisions resembling tattoos; others held a baby in their arms or carried it clutching their backs. Placed there by men separated from their wives, these figurines have been interpreted as evidence for the cult of Hathor, worshiped at Gebel Zeit as "Mistress of Galena" but also, as everywhere in Egypt, as goddess of fecundity and love.

EXPEDITIONS TO SINAI

Very early, beginning with the Third Dynasty, Sinai was the destination of important expeditions to bring back copper, malachite, and turquoise,

FIGURE 7.
Female figurine from the cult site at Gebel Zeit. Louvre E27257. © Ch. Larrieu-La Licorne. Photo courtesy of The Louvre.

the last highly valued for inlaid work and jewelry. In addition to the Egyptian personnel, there was a local work force of Semitic and Asiatic tribesmen recruited as interpreters and menial laborers. Rock inscriptions and commemorative stelae carved at Wadi Maghara and Serabit el-Khadim, the two major mining sites, record the members of the expeditions, which generally took place in winter, and their organization. Working conditions were harsh. The turquoise was mined in narrow, unventilated galleries; the camps were rudimentary, though the climate was glacial at the altitude of the mining areas; and water could be scarce. One inscription gives the figure of 734 Egyptians employed on an expedition; another speaks of six hundred donkeys transporting the equipment and provisions. Not all would return home, which was a good week's march away. The Sinai miners were volunteers. Their pay consisted in their being allowed to keep for their own profit some of the turquoise they mined; the remainder served to cover the expenses of the administration, security, and logistics from which they benefited. From the Middle Kingdom on, the exploitation of the mines occurred so regularly that at Serabit el-Khadim, the site most often visited, a grotto-sanctuary was constructed for the goddess Hathor, "Mistress of Turquoise." Situated halfway along the route leading up to the site, the pathway of Rud el-Air displays rocks covered with graffiti scrawled by exhausted miners who hastily inscribed their names while making a brief halt in the shadow of the mountain.

THE NILE AS TRANSPORT LINK

Most stone used in construction work was from quarries less difficult to reach, which were worked throughout the year. Sandstone was quarried from the cliffs of Gebel el-Silsila in Upper Egypt, which was close to the Nile and the waiting transport barges. The fine, smooth limestone blocks that encased the pyramids were extracted from the quarries of Tura and el-Masara, opposite Giza on the east bank of the Nile. As they removed the blocks from the cliffs, the workers created subterranean rooms and galleries more than 160 feet long. To transport the blocks of stone by boat, they either awaited the annual rise of the Nile waters or used the canal linking the Nile to the region of Dariut, where a port had been constructed at the foot of the plateau where the pyramids were situated. As for the enormous monoliths of red granite used in the interior chambers of the pyramids, they came from the quarries of Aswan and were also conveyed by boat.

To transport the blocks for Pharaoh's great construction works, the shipbuilders had to invent boats capable of bearing such heavy loads. The barges were made of cedar imported from the Lebanon; for local wood (acacia, sycamore) was not strong enough for such great vessels. In a bas-relief on the wall of the causeway leading up to the Fifth Dynasty pyramid of Wenis (c. 2460 B.C.E.) at Saqqara, there is a representation of the delivery of columns with palm-shaped capitals, extracted at Aswan for the pyramid complex. We see barges "loaded with granite columns of 20 cubits (more than 34 feet)"; each vessel carries two columns, which implies very deep water. In his autobiography, general Weni, a contemporary of King Pepy I (c. 2300) relates: "His Majesty sent me to Elephantine to bring back the red granite false door and its threshold, and the red granite portcullises and lintels, and to bring back the red granite doorways and flagstones of the upper chamber of the pyramid (whose name is) 'Merenre Appears in Perfection,' my mistress. They traveled downstream, thanks to me, to the pyramid 'Merenre Appears in Perfection' in six large boats — three barges and three boats of 80 cubits (more than 130 feet) — in a single expedition."

The Nile, which could be navigated without obstruction between Aswan and Giza, was a natural means of transport between the quarries and the construction works in progress. A good week was needed to make the journey, under the watchful eye of an expert pilot who knew how to avoid the sandbanks when the waters were low. The current of the river, which flowed from south to north, was favorable to these enterprises: once loaded, the boats traveled with the current, and there was scant need to ply the oars. The boats returned empty to the quarries, and the help of the north wind made the trip relatively effortless. To reconstruct the ancient Nile scene, we must imagine boats of various sizes plying the river in all directions (Figure 8). For the Nile was the country's natural transportation network: no bridge linked the east and west banks, so that the river was the only means of passage from one side to the other, and it was a unique and rapid artery for traveling south to north. Cruising it along with the heavy cargo boats loaded with stone were barges filled with the harvests on their way to the royal granaries, barques carrying pilgrims, pleasure boats, and the innumerable small crafts of the fishermen.

IMHOTEP, INVENTOR OF THE PYRAMID

At the royal residence, and for every peasant subject to corvée as well, the great event of a reign was of course the construction of Pharaoh's pyramid. Over the decades during the first half of the third millennium, the din

FIGURE 8.

Boat types:
(a) large traveling boat;
(b) small traveling boat;
(c) large cargo boat;
(d) small cargo boat.
From Old Kingdom
mastabas at Saqqara and
Giza.
After C. R. Lepsius,
Denkmaeler aus
Aegypten und
Aethiopien *(Berlin:*
Nicolai, *1849–56),*
Plates 45b, 43a, 62,
and 104b.

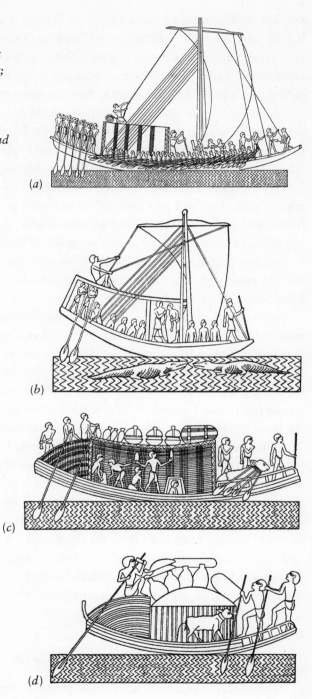

(a)

(b)

(c)

(d)

FIGURE 9.
Step pyramid of Djoser at Saqqara. Photo by Guillemette Andreu.

of the workshops where the stones were dressed, the cries of the workers, the dust, and the crowds scurrying about everywhere, invaded the limestone plateau extending northeast of Memphis which remains to this day the Seventh Wonder of the World.

The pyramid form originated in Egypt, in the innovative mind of Imhotep, the architect of Djoser (c. 2700 B.C.E.). Abandoning the light materials of brick and wood, he discovered how to make a tomb of stone for his king, one whose appearance would symbolize the ascent of the soul of the deceased to the powers of the sun and the sky (Figure 9). The six steps of Djoser's pyramid at Saqqara evoke a gigantic staircase or a petrified sunbeam descending onto the tomb to collect his soul and unite it with the divine sun. Henceforth, all the pharaohs of Egypt would be buried in pyramids, until the beginning of the New Kingdom (c. 1552), when the capital was moved to Thebes and the sovereigns broke with a millennium-old tradition, choosing the rock-cut tombs of the Valley of the Kings as their burial places. From Abu Rawash north of Giza to Dahshur south of Saqqara, the enormous silhouettes of more than thirty pyramids loom over the sun-baked desert, constituting the most impressive archaeological and aesthetic spectacle of any visit to the land of the pharaohs and leaving the beholder with an impression of absolute eternity.

Unfortunately, archaeologists have no contemporary representation of the construction of a pyramid. Though the establishment and management of the construction site fell under his responsibility, no vizier commissioned a representation of pyramid building in progress on the walls of his tomb. Nor has any diagram or text on papyrus been found concerning the great project, as is the case for the tombs of the Valley of the Kings in the New Kingdom. The study of texts, so often the primary tool in Egyptological work, is of no help in reconstructing the stages of the construction of these monuments. One can only investigate the stones on the ground to understand, through research, how they ended up as pyramids. Beginning in 1926, the French archaeologist Jean-Philippe Lauer pursued just this mission. Year after year, he explored the site of Saqqara, progressively reconstructing the pyramid complex of Djoser and, through his patience, becoming an intimate of Imhotep himself.

THE FIRST VISIT TO THE CONSTRUCTION SITE

The first step was the choice of a site. The king, accompanied by his vizier and his architect, established the location of his future home, its size, and its orientation. We know that the plateau of Giza, renowned for its three Great Pyramids, was chosen for its ability to withstand the burden imposed by the mass of the construction and for its proximity to the high waters of the inundation. Less than a thousand yards separated the construction site from the harbor area where the blocks coming from the quarry at Tura were unloaded. Moreover, not all the stones had to be brought from elsewhere; the immediate environs of Giza furnished the majority of the blocks needed for the masonry of the interior. Once the king had made up his mind, it was necessary to plan the construction work: the number of stone blocks needed and where they would be extracted, the requisitioning of the work force, and the location of villages for the workmen near the site. The plans for the monument were drawn up by the architect, who was also "overseer of the royal scribes and overseer of the works of the king." Some architects have left their names. Besides Imhotep, whom posterity quickly recognized as a genius and who was deified in the popular religion of the first millennium, we know of Nefermaat and his son Hemiunu, who designed the plans for the pyramid of Snofru at Maidum and the famous pyramid of Khufu at Giza. In the Fifth and Sixth Dynasties, successive generations of the Senedjemib family of architects designed a goodly number of royal pyramids.

THE CONSTRUCTION OF THE PYRAMID

At the site, the ground was smoothed and leveled, the work done with infinite care: from one side to the other, the base of Khufu's pyramid, the biggest of them all, differs in level by less than eight-tenths of an inch. North was determined by astronomical observation, enabling the geometers to align the four sides quite precisely to the cardinal points. The exact outline of the pyramid's area could then be marked out on the ground. For the pyramid of Khufu, it was decided that each side would be exactly 440 cubits, or 755.6464 feet. Once the position had been outlined on the ground, the king returned to conduct the foundation ritual, the "stretching of the cord," which would consecrate the building and place it under the protection of the gods. The goddess Seshat, patroness of intellectual occupations — calculation and the written archives of the plans of temples — presided over the ceremony. In the course of the ritual, the king himself planted four stakes at the corners of the monument, joining them with a cord. Next, he threw a handful of sand on the surface area and solemnly laid the first stone. The workmen then took over. To fill in the 91,806,000 cubic feet of the pyramid of Khufu, they had to quarry and lay nearly 2,500,000 stone blocks, each weighing approximately two and a half tons. When the funerary chamber designed to receive the royal sarcophagus was subterranean, they began by constructing this portion of the monument and then erected the various elements of the superstructure. The limestone blocks, extracted from the neighboring quarries with the help of levers, were positioned in level courses, then adjusted into position with the help of stone splinters or clay mortar. To raise the first courses, ramps of mud were positioned on each side; the workers hauled the blocks up these ramps, gliding them along on sleds. About seventy men were needed to drag a block weighing two and a half tons. As the monument rose, the operation became progressively more difficult. Lauer imagines that above the level of eighty-two feet, a single ramp with a slight incline was used, built against one side of the pyramid. The work was thus carried out on each of the sides in succession, concluding with the exterior surface, which was cased with the beautiful limestone from Tura. Although the blocks of the interior masonry could be cut with no great precision, these exterior blocks were worked with care. The stonecutters took out their T squares and plumb lines to deliver stone blocks of equal size with perfectly horizontal surfaces. When the four duly encased faces finally met at the desired height, after so many years of labor, they were crowned with the granite pyramidion that marked the utmost peak of the monument. Then the workers began to dismantle the access ramps, all the while polishing the blocks of the facade from top to bottom, so that the royal tomb would gleam in the sunlight.

Khufu's father Snofru must not have turned from the step pyramid to the true pyramid form without hesitation; for archaeologists attribute to him three successive pyramids, at Maidum and Dahshur. According to the German archaeologist Rainer Stadelmann, two to three years were needed to raise fifteen courses of stone blocks for Snofru's pyramid at Dahshur, and Lauer estimates that the completion of the one at Maidum took between eight and eleven years. The Greek historian Herodotus (fifth century B.C.E.) proposes the figure of one hundred thousand men, taking twenty years, to erect the Great Pyramid of Khufu. On the whole, the pyramids of the Old Kingdom are the biggest and best built and thus the best preserved. Those of the pharaohs of the Middle Kingdom, at el-Lahun, Hawara, and el-Lisht, are today no more than enormous heaps of bricks and limestone destroyed by time.

THE LIFE OF THE WORKERS

To keep the construction effort running smoothly all year round without interfering with agricultural work, teams of about twenty thousand men were rotated every three or four months. The work week was nine days, with the tenth devoted to leisure. The workmen took advantage of their free day to return home to see their families or simply to wash their clothes and make their bread for the coming week. Remains of workshops, storehouses, and shacks have been unearthed in the vicinity of the pyramids of Giza. Each hut was designed to shelter a dozen workers and had a kitchen, a cellar, and an oven for baking. Administration and provisioning were carried out by an army of scribes who kept a close watch over the deliveries of water, grain, clothing, and tools. Tombs of workers who died laboring on the pyramid were discovered in 1992 by Egyptian archaeologists at the southeast of the Giza plateau. Study of their skeletons has revealed that all the men suffered serious pathologies of the spinal column and coccyx from the excessive strain of hauling and carrying.

The pyramid was not the only construction underway. For it to function effectively and thus enable the cult of the deceased king to be carried out, it was necessary to surround it with an enclosure wall; to build a second, small "satellite" pyramid; and to add two temples. The lower, or valley

FIGURE 10.
The Great Sphinx and the pyramid of Khephren at Giza.
Photo by Guillemette Andreu.

temple, was reserved for the embalming ritual and the more ordinary funerary practices; the upper temple, which adjoined the pyramid, was where the
priesthood carried out the royal cult after the burial of the king. Between
the two, a sloping causeway enabled processions to bring their daily funerary offerings.

The renowned Sphinx of Giza (page xii and Figure 10) was sculpted
from the same limestone rock that crops out at the level of the lower temple
of the pyramid of Khephren. We know there was a natural rock feature
there which was especially prominent and undoubtedly considered un-
sightly. And so the idea of modeling a majestic sphinx with the head of the
king, turned toward the rising sun, was born in the minds of architects and
sculptors to whom nothing ever seemed impossible.

4 SCRIBES AND SCHOLARS

During the first centuries of the third millennium, as the Egyptians were organizing the political, religious, and economic life of their land, they recognized their need for a system of written notation for their language. Within a few decades, hieroglyphic writing became the single, regular means of rendering the semantic and phonetic contents of the language spoken on the banks of the Nile and of the rituals carried out there. Various dialects must have existed in a population so diverse at the outset and scattered over a ribbon of land 630 miles long, but it seems evident that this regularization imposed by writing occurred to their detriment. If we recall that five major dialects have been identified in Coptic, the last stage of the pharaonic language, written and spoken in Egypt in the Christian era, there is every reason to think that dialects, or vernaculars, abounded in earlier periods. Linguists of the twentieth century have sought to detect, in texts discovered in Lower Egypt, idioms specific to that region which one would not find in texts found elsewhere, in the valley. But such results are deceptive; for they tend rather to show that our evidence for the written language, from the earliest texts on, constitutes the notation of a language in the process of unification, symbol of the political and religious will of the guardians of writing. This creation of the scribes was wholly concentrated on the demand made of them: that they invent and perfect a means of setting down, in a way that all the literate could read, the cosmologic and pharaonic laws of the nation being born. The written language coincided with the official language that emanated from the temples and the offices of the state, promulgating the commands and the discourse that worked together to build a homogeneous culture. That is why the possession of writing was always considered the sign of the transmission of power and knowledge; a parallel could be drawn between the use of this normative language developed by the Egyptian scribes in their writings and what was done with Latin in medieval Europe. The evolution of the writing system and the variations that can be observed result from the period of the texts, their nature, and their medium: a religious text carved in stone would be written in a more traditional language than a rough draft scribbled on a potsherd.

THE HIEROGLYPHIC WRITING SYSTEM: KEY TO POWER AND PRIVILEGE

In the Old Kingdom, knowledge of hieroglyphic writing was at first the privilege of the ruling class, which played a leading role in both lay society and the ranks of the clergy. Priestly office presupposed the acquisition of this sacred knowledge and the capacity to communicate messages from the gods under the protection of Thoth, the patron of scribes. Thus, around 2200 B.C.E., Djau was "scribe of the divine book-rolls, director of scribes of the royal documents, and chief lector priest." Scribes of lesser status, who did not know the beautiful hieroglyphic script but only the cursive, nonpictorial hieratic, were given administrative and practical jobs. The titulary of Kaaper, who lived around 2400, indicates that he was "scribe of the administration, scribe of the pasturing of spotted cows, inspector of the scribes of the state, scribe of state documents, and scribe of royal expeditions." None of these responsibilities implied the daily use of hieroglyphs carved in stone; without doubt, his duties were limited to recording administrative documents in hieratic. In the Middle Kingdom, the political situation of the land had changed. After the great social upheaval that shook Egypt during the First Intermediate Period (2200–2060), the state felt the need to restore a sound and effective administration and placed its trust in a rising middle class, a veritable beehive of scribal civil servants ready to serve their country. Thus over time, the knowledge of hieroglyphs ceased to be the prerogative of the nobility and became the distinctive sign of a social class in quest of prestige and devoted to the state.

By his very abilities, the literate man was put in charge of other workers. A bourgeois from the delta named Khety, who lived in the Middle Kingdom, took his son to the scribal school maintained at Pharaoh's court. On the way, he painted a totally negative picture of manual labor and exalted the status of scribes, trying thus to encourage his son to submit obediently to the apprenticeship awaiting him. This text, known by the title of the "Satire of the Trades," remained famous in the schools and became the classic exercise for budding scribes, who learned it by heart and practiced copying passages from it: "I shall make you love books more than your mother, I shall make you see their beauty, for it is greater than that of any other calling. . . . What I am doing in taking you to the Residence, I do it for love of you. A single day at school is (already) profitable to you, and the work one does there is as eternal as the mountains. . . . There is no trade without a boss, except for that of the scribe, who himself bosses."

The instruction awaiting the young boy would make him, at the end of his schooling, "a capable scribe, able with his hands, with clean fingers," and at the same time a man well adjusted to the established order and respectful of its rules, knowing how to remain silent and speak at the right moment. In the Egyptian moral code, knowledge and virtue were inseparable. They were the acknowledged qualities of the scribe, who in the course of his studies immersed himself in the maxims of Egyptian wisdom literature, the source of irreproachable conduct. The instructional treatise of Ptahhotpe, mayor and vizier of King Izezi of the Fifth Dynasty, states: "Speak when you know you have a solution, it is the sage who will speak in council. . . . Be prudent when you speak, so as to say things that count. Then the officials who hear will say, 'How good is what comes from his mouth!' " Through the mediation of teachers and of wisdom texts whose authors were educators, the traditional ethic was handed down from generation to generation, and respect was maintained for the duty and stability instituted by Maat.

THE SCRIBAL SCHOOL

Entering school around the age of ten, the young Egyptian began his apprenticeship in writing by copying whole phrases in the cursive hieroglyphs we call the hieratic script. He used ostraca as a notebook for his drafts. Papyrus was too rare and expensive to be wasted at school; it was reserved for the liturgical and administrative texts written by professionals. From the New Kingdom, we have several examples of wooden tablets that were washed after being corrected by the teacher. The pupil memorized what he copied, recopied it on the back of his tablet or on some other medium, and then showed his work to his teacher. The master neither broke down the signs for him nor showed him the ideograms in which the hieratic signs or ligatures had their origin. This knowledge of the hieroglyph in its complete, pictorial form was the second stage of schooling, permitting access to the writing system of important texts and to the carvings on monuments.

Discipline was quite strict. Every lesson began with the reminder "Be attentive and hear my speech. Forget nothing of what I say to you." Attentiveness was constantly demanded. Moreover, we may note that in the Egyptian vocabulary, the same verb *sedjem* means "to hear" and "to obey" and that it is written with the ideogram of the ear, the prerequisite organ for attention. Again, Khety says to his son, "The one who hears becomes someone distinguished." Any kind of persuasion could be used to encourage the pupil to work: compliments, the promise of an envied future exempt from the hard labor of the corvée, competition, threats, and finally, corporal punishment when the pupil turned out to be exceptionally lazy or undisciplined.

Once out of school, the adolescent was apprenticed to a professional scribe. The latter could be his own father, or a close relative, who would train him for his future profession, instill in him a basic knowledge of administration, and teach him the formats and polite formulas of documents. If he proved suitable for the "socioprofessional" milieu intended for him, the young man was called on to succeed his teacher and pursue his career: "Emulate your father and your ancestors. . . . Their words are written in books; open them, read them, and try to make this knowledge yours, for wisdom appears to you, freed of its dross."

THE SCRIBE AT WORK

Representations of scribes at work are quite numerous in the Old Kingdom, both in the statuary and on the walls of mastabas (see Figures 11, 15, 22, and 26). Always present to record the cattle and the harvest, the scribe and his assistants took part in the economic life of the estates. The hieroglyph employed in writing the words for *scribe* and for the act of writing is none other than the scribe's palette. We should note here that the word "scribe," when feminine in gender, designates the profession of "make-up artist," which indicates that knowledge of the art of drawing and painting was implicit in the act of writing hieroglyphs.

The scribe's equipment consisted of a wooden palette with two small wells hollowed into it, one for his red ocher pigment and the other for his black carbon pigment (see Figure 26), along with a little pot to hold water and a case containing one or more pens, the little stalks of rush that he used for writing. Sometimes the palette was replaced by a mother-of-pearl shell that the scribe balanced on his knee as he sat cross-legged and wrote. The most valued material was papyrus, which could be rolled up without cracking and washed without damage, and on which beautiful hieroglyphs could easily be drawn. No representation of a scribe at work shows him writing on ostraca. From the significant number of ostraca discovered at archaeological sites, we know that they were widely used to make rough drafts and copies, but we understand that this medium was never considered to be a writing material worthy of the noble profession of scribe.

The craft of papyrus making can be confirmed from the very beginning of pharaonic Egypt. The tomb of Hemaka, a high official of the First Dynasty, at the beginning of the third millennium B.C.E., contained a roll of papyrus, unfortunately blank. Growing from an umbelliferous plant that was plentiful on the banks of the Nile and in the marshes, papyrus stalks could attain a height exceeding sixteen feet. They were torn off when they were at their most supple and cut into sections of equal length, about sixteen inches, which determined the height of the written page. The sections were sliced into thin strips, which were set side by side on a board, parallel to one another, and pounded smooth with a hammer. Then a second layer was placed at a right angle on top of the first one, and the two were moistened and pressed together; the sap of the plant, diluted with the water, glued the strips to one another. When every trace of moisture had evaporated, the sheet was ready — smooth, white, and supple. To make a roll of papyrus, the operation was repeated several times, and the resulting sheets were glued together in the same way. About twenty sheets, sixteen inches high by sixteen inches wide, made a medium sized roll.

The scribe usually worked on a mat, sitting cross-legged or squatting, with his roll set on his knees. First he wrote on the inside of the roll, and then he turned it over to continue his text on the verso. On papyrus, the direction of writing was always from right to left, though texts carved in stone, in temples or on statues, could also be oriented from left to right, either in columns or in lines. Black ink was most often used, red being reserved for titles, chapter headings, the first words of phrases, and punctuation marks. The same use of red ink is to be found in the rubrics of manuscripts made by Western copyists in the Middle Ages.

The scribe stored his equipment in a wooden box that he carried to his workplace. He always had one or two spare pens stuck behind his ear, ready in case the one he was using gave out. When his work was done, he affixed his seal to the raw clay that would seal his document. The Pyramid

Texts depict the scribe's activity thus: "He opens his chests of papyrus, breaks the seals of his decrees, seals his papyrus rolls, and dispatches his tireless messengers."

We have no representations of girls writing, but we know that princesses could read. Moreover, to get a letter or an administrative document written, Egyptians could call on their village's public scribe, whose services were for hire by the very many who were illiterate. Indeed, it is estimated that in the age of the pyramids, fewer then 5 percent of Egypt's population could read and write.

GREAT LITERATURE

From the Old Kingdom on, princes and rulers understood that writing ought also to be employed for purely literary ends: though religious literature and the compiling of rituals could not be neglected, readers need not be deprived of the good stories that could spring from the inventive minds of the best scribes. Though they were amateurs at literature and great books, men of letters produced a genuine fictional literature that has its place in anthologies of world literature from all ages. Besides religious texts and the moral precepts intended for schoolboys, Egyptologists have reconstructed numerous texts in which adventure, suspense, psychology, and good and bad intentions successfully alternate. These novels and popular tales were handed down from generation to generation, enduring through the centuries in the collective memory and ever again delighting a new public. Still, much of this literature has been lost. For example, the "Book of Kemyt" (the "Summa") is known from more than four hundred copies, every one of which is far from complete! Authors are rarely known; for modesty and self-effacement were considered proper. Working on an official commission emanating from the palace, an artist would not sign a book any more than he would a statue.

NOVELS AND TALES

The Middle Kingdom was the golden age of Egyptian literature. At that time, the language reached a degree of maturity that permitted unlimited expression with the nuances required by poetry or realism. Moreover, it was this stage of the language that would remain the traditional Egyptian, the classical form of the written language, until the Late Period.

The most famous work of the Middle Kingdom is the "Story of Sinuhe," justly considered the "first novel" in the history of world literature. Legend has it that Rudyard Kipling had it on his bedside table. We read in it the fantastic adventures of a court favorite of Pharaoh Amenemhet I, at the beginning of the second millennium B.C.E. For obscure reasons, he took flight at the death of his king and experienced an extraordinary destiny in Asia, where he took a wife and waged war with desert sheikhs. Though he became an important personage, homesickness tormented him. At the end of the novel, the new king of Egypt summoned him back to court and showered him with glory. Our hero would spend a happy old age on the banks of the Nile, endlessly regaling astounded courtiers with the extravagant tale of his wanderings.

The "Story of the Shipwrecked Sailor" also enjoyed great favor with the Egyptian public. It recounts the epic adventure of a sailor who, as the only survivor of the shipwreck of his boat, found himself on the Isle of Ka, a mythical and marvelous island whose prince was a gigantic serpent. The island turned out to be a paradise abounding in incense and food; its master, the serpent, welcomed the sailor with sumptuous gifts and words of comfort. When a ship came to fetch the stranded sailor, the island sank into the waters. With the "Story of the Shipwrecked Sailor," Egyptian literature touches on a classic theme in Mediterranean and eastern lands, the seafaring epic, which is also to be found in the *Epic of Gilgamesh*, the *Odyssey*, and *Sinbad the Sailor*.

The "Story of the Eloquent Peasant" must have struck the fancy of Egyptians with its endless talk and sophisticated arguments. It depicts an unfortunate man from the countryside who went down to the city to sell the produce of his plot of land. Along the way, a scoundrel robbed him of his donkeys and his goods and left him helpless at the side of the road. The peasant lodged a complaint with a high state dignitary. Impressed by the plaintiff's eloquence, the official dragged out the proceedings so as to amuse himself listening to the arguments the peasant would endlessly develop. Nine successive pleas ensue on this papyrus of more than four hundred lines, in which we see the poor man having recourse to all the artifices of rhetoric to win his case at the end of the story. Justice was done, the oppressed man was avenged, and the moral code remained intact.

How to save Pharaoh from boredom: this was the subject of the short stories contained in Papyrus Westcar, which was written around 1830 B.C.E. King Khufu summoned his son in order to hear his distracting stories and alleviate the sad atmosphere reigning in his palace. There were many marvels in his tales portraying magicians who could perform miracles, and the stories were so astonishing that the pharaoh forgot his melancholy. The theme of royal diversion is dear to Orientals; we encounter it again centuries later in the stories of the *Thousand and One Nights*, in which the beautiful Scheherazade would make up extraordinary stories to distract the sultan Shahriyar from his boredom.

Undoubtedly written in the same period, the "Story of Neferkare and General Sisene" is especially farcical. An amateur detective applies himself to denouncing the nocturnal activities of a fictitious pharaoh named Neferkare. Leaving the palace furtively, this king goes to the house of his general in the middle of the night, climbs a ladder to his bedroom, spends four hours there, and returns to the palace incognito. The story leaves us to understand that the relations between the two men were homosexual in nature, which was evidently not very appropriate for this demigod of a pharaoh.

PESSIMISTIC LITERATURE

Egyptian literature presents an image of a rather gay and sociable people in love with wit and pleasantries. Yet in the First Intermediate Period (2200–2060 B.C.E.), after the social troubles that profoundly shook the country at the end of the Old Kingdom, a "pessimistic" literature emanated from the minds of scribes, still in dread of the moral and political chaos that had touched them. In a text describing the thoroughly abominable state into which the land had fallen, the sage Ipuwer laments, "Lo, the women are sterile, for one no longer conceives. . . . Lo, hearts are violent, and misfortune spreads through the land. . . . Lo, great ones go hungry . . . but servants are served." This same tone is to be found in the "Prophecy of Neferty," a text predicting the misfortunes that might overwhelm Egypt in the event of revolution: "One demands bread with blood . . . a man kills his own father . . . the goods of one man are taken away and given to another who comes from outside."

Preserved on a single papyrus of the Twelfth Dynasty (1991–1785 B.C.E.), the "Dialogue of a Man Weary of Life with His Soul" is the most moving example of this pessimistic literature. We read there the metaphysical discussion undertaken with his soul by a man who is tired of living: "To whom can I speak today? Brothers are wicked, and today's friends no longer love. To whom can I speak today? Hearts are greedy, and everyone carries off his neighbor's goods. . . . To whom can I speak today? One is satisfied with evil, and goodness is cast to the ground everywhere. . . . To whom can I speak today? The criminal is the one who is loved. . . . To whom can I speak today? There are no longer just men, the land is abandoned to evildoers. . . . To whom can I speak today? I am burdened with misery, without a friend. . . . Death is before me today like a cure for a sick man, like recovery from an accident." At the end of this litany of disenchanted reflections, the man, overwhelmed by loneliness, sees no way out but suicide. His soul then answers him, urging him to renew his trust in the gods and in his own destiny, until the moment of his natural death, which would occur in good time.

Inscribed for the first time in the tomb of King Inyotef of the Eleventh Dynasty, at the beginning of the second millennium B.C.E., the "Harper's Song" stemmed from the same current of skepticism as the preceding text and quickly became the classic refrain of the banquets depicted on tomb walls. Doubts and questions are posed just as keenly, but the proposed solution is different. As death is inevitable, one might as well avail oneself of the present and "spend a happy day": "May she whom you love be seated beside you, may there be singing and dancing before you. Cast care far from you, think of rejoicing, until there comes the day of mooring at the land that loves silence."

THE WISDOM GENRE

We would like to be able to extol by name the authors of the world's most ancient literature, but the only ones we know are those who wrote the wisdom texts, those maxims and precepts on the art of living which played so important a role in the education of young scribes and, through them, in the establishment of a strict ethical code. Presented as instructive advice from experienced sages to young people, fathers to their sons, or reigning pharaohs to their future successors, these texts are always signed and usually begin with the phrase "Beginning of the instruction made by X to state a message of truth to his son Y." The first of these teachers was Imhotep, the famous architect of King Djoser of the Third Dynasty (c. 2700 B.C.E.), whose moral and intellectual charisma was so influential that he was deified in the first millennium. Prince Hardjedef, son of Khufu of the Fourth Dynasty (c. 2600), reminded his son of the need to "found a household and take a hearty woman to wife, so that a son will be born" to him. Next to write his maxims was the vizier Ptahhotpe, in the time of King Izezi. These are essentially advice on how to live in discretion, modesty, equity, and respect for others.

With only one exception, the authors of wisdom texts in the Middle Kingdom were aging pharaohs desirous of leaving good instructions on the "way of life" to their successors. Literature and politics are totally mingled in these didactic texts, whose object is to clarify and exalt the authority of the king. Only Khety, the bourgeois from the delta who took his son to the school at court, wrote pedagogic advice unmarked by a preoccupation with royal propaganda. His "Satire of the Trades" is essentially a critique of manual labor, added to an overdone praise of the bureaucrat's position.

AN ABUNDANT CORRESPONDENCE

There are choice examples of the epistolary genre in Egyptian literature. From the Old Kingdom on, letters with a set format and customary formulas can be read on fragments of papyrus. Beginning with the Middle Kingdom, the drafting of a typical letter was one of the basic exercises in the scribal schools, and the teachers knew by heart a whole series of models applicable to various situations.

The reading of correspondence exchanged between the royal residence and the various local authorities, between the vizier and his subordinates, or between two government departments is a major source of useful information on the administration of Egypt. By chance, complete papyri preserve these letters, often copied and recopied, and disclose the workings of government. Their tone is usually friendly, their polite formulas much longer than the subject matter of the letter. But missives written in scathing terms are sometimes encountered. Thus the official Pepy, furious at the return of his superior to the city of el-Lahun, addressed a threatening letter to him: "This is a communication regarding what was said to your humble servant: 'The master . . . returned to (the Residence) in the fourth month of Shemu, day 10.' What a shame that you have returned safe and sound! . . . The spirit of the overseer of the temple of the ruler, Pepy, has taken action against you . . . forever and ever and ever! . . . May you be slaughtered!"

The most enjoyable letters come from family archives; for they reveal the ties and interests uniting people under the same roof. They also add considerably to our knowledge of the private affairs of ordinary people. Heqanakhte, a Theban farmer sent on a mission to the north in the reign of Mentuhotpe Sankhkare at the end of the third millennium, attempted to manage his agricultural estate by courier. In his letters we read orders concerning the schedule of cultivation, the distribution or renting of fields, and the arbitration of household quarrels. Heqanakhte's correspondence portrays his family and the personnel of his farmstead, letting us imagine the intrigues and conflicts in their relationships. We even read personal letters: "It is a girl who addresses her mother, it is Zatnebsekhtu who addresses Zatnebsekhtu. A thousand wishes for life, prosperity, and health! May you prosper! May Hathor satisfy you for love of me. Have no care for me, all is well. . . . Take care that Gereg does not neglect that about which I spoke to him. And greet all the household, in life, prosperity, and health." The Heqanakhte archive contains so many spicy details and presents so many endearing characters that it inspired Agatha Christie's detective novel *Death Comes as the End*, whose plot unfolds on the banks of the Nile.

SCIENCE AND MATHEMATICS

It is also in Egyptian texts that we find the earliest traces of scientific research. From the Old Kingdom on, scholars conducted experiments and made fundamental discoveries, which they recorded in treatises that would be improved over the centuries but always consulted. Scholars and priests tirelessly drew up lists of significant objects or events from nature or society. Comparison of these data and analysis of the observed phenomena permitted the formulation of scientific hypotheses, particularly in mathematics, astronomy, and medicine. Egyptian science was founded on the principle that the world, as conceived by the creator gods, was knowable. The cosmic order and the laws of nature were governed by Maat, a notion designating the perfect equilibrium established by the gods and maintained by the reigning pharaoh. Scientific practice therefore consisted above all in understanding Maat and proposing systems and means of serving and respecting it. Science conformed to religion; it never conflicted with it. When the human mind reached the limits of demonstrated knowledge, there was recourse to myth.

Our decimal system goes back to the impressive wave of discoveries that sprang from the minds of Egyptian scholars at the beginning of the third millennium B.C.E. Undoubtedly, it originated in the fact that people have ten fingers, which they use to count. Specific hieroglyphic signs denote units, tens, hundreds, and thousands, permitting all the arithmetical operations; these were often required homework for schoolboys, alternating with their labors at writing. Fractions were complicated by the fact that only the numerator 1 was known, along with ⅔, ¾, ⅘, and ⅚. All calculations had therefore to be presented as a series of fractions with decreasing denominators. Measurements were made in royal cubits, which equaled 20.61 inches. One hundred cubits made a *khet*, and 10,000 square cubits constituted a *setjat*, often mentioned in calculations of areas.

ASTRONOMY

Astronomical knowledge was based on observation of the sky and its constellations, to which priests devoted themselves on the rooftops of their temples. At a very early date they succeeded in establishing an annual calendar that is the very source of our own. The beginning of their year coincided with the heliacal rising of the Dog Star, Sirius, around July 19 in our calendar, which was the first day of the Inundation in Egypt. The concomitance of the two phenomena, one solar and the other hydrologic, sufficed to induce the idea of a new year in the minds of the Egyptians, the *weprenpet* that began with the new moon of the month of July. The year was divided into thirty-six decans of ten days, making 360 days, to which five extra days were added at the end. Lending an extraordinary character to these "epagomenal" days, mythology styled them the birthdays of the gods Osiris, Horus, and Seth and of the goddesses Isis and Nephthys. A month was composed of three decans, and four months made up a season. The only failure of the Egyptian astronomers lay in not contriving the leap year, so that the year they devised regularly lacked a quarter of a day. The progressive discrepancy between the real year and their civil year amounted to about one month per century. One had to wait 1,460 years for the heliacal rising of Sothis to coincide once again with the first day of Inundation. The astronomers were aware of this enormous interval, which they called the "Sothic cycle."

The Egyptians distinguished stars grouped in constellations from the planets, which they called "the unwearying stars." Five planets were recognized: Mars, Saturn, Jupiter, Venus, and Mercury. To determine north and the other cardinal points, so important in the orientation of pyramids and sacred buildings, astronomers had to sight the middle of the ellipse formed by the maximum deviation of one of the stars of the Big Dipper. The polestar of the Little Dipper could not be used; for the earth's axis was not aligned on that star in the time of the pyramids.

We owe the division of the day into twenty-four hours to the Egyptians.

Their hours, however, varied in length with the season: in summer, the hours of the night were very short because darkness did not last for an actual twelve hours, but the hours of the day were quite long.

MEDICINE

The most highly educated scribes and priests formed the elite of the medical corps. From earliest times, on the walls of Old Kingdom mastabas, physicians appear as a structured guild, organized into various specialties. We encounter general practitioners, ophthalmologists, dentists, and surgeons. Their profession had several ranks, ranging from intern to physician-in-chief, who could have the honor of becoming chief doctor of the palace, assigned to the person of the king. Physicians were highly appreciated at court and by the nobility, but country people preferred their village witch doctor, who would try to comfort the sick with his arsenal of magical spells and potions.

Papyrus Ebers, written around 1600 B.C.E., is a compilation of the seven hundred medical prescriptions devised by physicians since the birth of their profession, classified by illnesses and the organs concerned. Papyrus Smith is a surgical treatise, principally concerned with the care of wounds and fractures. Egyptians' knowledge of anatomy was empirical: the dissection of human cadavers was forbidden for religious reasons, so they could not take advantage of the mummification process to acquaint themselves with human physiology. Physicians were therefore ignorant of the kidneys, and they connected the stomach to the lung and the lung to the heart, which they considered the center of the organism. Papyrus Ebers states: "Beginning of the secret of the physician; knowledge of the workings of the heart and knowledge of the heart itself. There are vessels in it that go to each limb. When the physician . . . places his fingers on the head, the neck, the hands, the heart itself, the arms, the legs, or any part whatsoever, he finds the heart, for its vessels go to each member." It continues, explaining that the heart carries blood in its arteries, along with tears, urine, sperm, air (which enters it through the nose), food, and fecal matter.

To identify the illnesses that struck the ancient Egyptians, we can turn to their medical books for an endless list. Today this information is augmented by research on skeletons and mummies by paleopathologists working at archaeological sites, who furnish valuable information on the health and hygiene of the Egyptian people. Tuberculosis, smallpox, and polio were common, as well as tetanus and parasitic diseases such as schistosomiasis.

Many people suffered from arthritis of the joints, and some from arterio-sclerosis. Cancer has been detected in a man around forty years of age, discovered in the cemetery of Nag el-Deir (c. 2200 B.C.E.), but most tumors were benign.

The remedies offered in the texts are of all sorts: pills, potions, massages, dressings, ointments, poultices, eye drops, gargling, inhalations, enemas. The plant world, with its herbs reputed to be medicinal, furnished the bulk of the material for these drugs, but physicians also turned without hesitation to a pharmacopoeia of animal, mineral, even excremental origin. A good medicine could be made up of a complex mixture of meat, fat, and blood, milk, animal feces, clumps of mud, and powdered leaves and roots.

DENTISTS AND MAGICIANS

Teeth were cared for by specialists. They made fillings with a poor mixture of resin and malachite, fashioned bridges by tying teeth together with gold or silver wire, and drained abscesses by perforating the jawbone. As for eyes, which were constantly assaulted by dust and poor hygiene, preparations of warm drops were made to combat trachoma and cataracts. We can doubt the effectiveness of the remedies invented by the physicians of ancient Egypt, but nonetheless, we know that their surgeons obtained fine results, especially in bone operations, the suturing of wounds, and the setting of fractures.

When the physician experienced a setback or was unable to treat, the magician took over. Magic was very much present in the practices of the Egyptian people, for it alone could attack the root of the disease and eradicate it from the patient's body. Illness meant that a person had fallen victim to the hostility of a demon, an evil spirit, or a ghost. With his talismans and his incantations, the magician could ward off the evil eye and combat these malevolent spirits. Drawing on episodes of Egyptian mythology in which a god was seen obtaining the cure his own patient required, the magician implored the protection of that very deity to drive out the evil. The texts do not specify his success rate.

5 ARTS, CRAFTS, AND TRADES

During the three thousand years of its existence and semantic evolution, the language of the hieroglyphic texts never made the distinction between an artist and an artisan. A single ideogram, representing the metal tool used in cutting stone vases, designated all manual activity requiring the skill of an artist or artisan. This tells us that pharaonic culture did not conceive the modern notion of art for art's sake, or the creation of a statue or the execution of a painting as the intentional creation of beauty. The objects and remains of ancient Egypt evoke such admiration and rapture in the modern viewer that we can lose sight of this fundamental absence of an aesthetic will in their artistic production. Not least of the Egyptians' accomplishments during the age of the pyramids is that the archaeological evidence of their civilization includes master works of the first rank in the history of world art, though that was not their original purpose. Nevertheless, we must not hastily conclude that they lacked a taste for the Beautiful, even if that was a secondary concern.

ART IN THE SERVICE OF ETERNITY

The avowed goal of the artist-artisans was to put all their know-how at the service of duration and eternity. Their efforts and their achievements were supposed to be applied to this master plan. Whether in building temples for their gods or in carving statues of individuals, their task was first and foremost to eternalize the actual, to assist humanity in integrating itself into the cosmic order and gaining immortality. The artist contributed to the preservation of life by approaching it as closely as possible, whatever the reality he had to represent. If we visit the rooms dedicated to statuary in a collection of Egyptian art, we never fail to be staggered by the realistic character of the glance, the smile, or the often unique expression of the figures, and we sometimes believe we are face to face with a rigorous portrait, a "photograph" realized in stone or wood. In the Cairo Museum there is an Old Kingdom statue to which Auguste Édouard Mariette's workmen gave the Arabic name Sheikh el-Beled, "Village Mayor," at the time of its discovery at Saqqara in 1860. It represents a plump individual, whose neck has been thickened by age and stoutness. His face and his eyes—emphasized by their pupils of black stone inlaid in alabaster — are so vivaciously animated that the workmen, struck by the resemblance to the mayor of their village, believed they were looking at his fossilized double and fled in terror. The famous seated scribe in the Louvre (Figure 11), with his concentrated expression and striking gaze, is the perfect portrait of an accomplished man who has "made it."

These works, many of which achieve their goal, were born of a desire to prolong life beyond the existence of the biologic creature, of a will to immortalize thought and spirituality, and of a horror of the ephemeral. The message of the Egyptians, who were concerned above all with eternity, has come down through the ages and reached us.

ARTISTIC CONVENTIONS

The motive of absolute realism also engendered principles of representing reality based on combining points of view, especially in relief and painting. It was deemed necessary to show beings as they really are, in full, and not as they appear. Thus to render the most complete possible view of a human being, the artist represented an eye and the shoulders in frontal view, while privileging the profile of the face, because the nose, so represented, was considered one of the more pregnant features of a personality. To render a pleasure garden from all sides, the pool was shown from above, the trees surrounding it frontally, and the birds in profile, thus making the absence of perspective a deliberate principle. The respective size of people and things was the object of a strict canon: the pharaoh and the gods were larger than courtiers, who in turn were larger than ordinary people or enemies. These conventions ruled the practices of Egyptian draftsmen and the work of artistic studios for more than three thousand years, with almost no exceptions. It is undoubtedly this absolute fidelity to a system of represen-

FIGURE 11.
Statue of seated scribe. Louvre E3023. © Chuzeville. Photo courtesy of The Louvre.

tation established once and for all at the beginning of pharaonic history that engenders an impression of homogeneity, stability, and serenity in the modern viewer, though it can also seem oppressive in its conformity.

UNSIGNED WORKS

The creators of these works — architects, sculptors, painters, draftsmen, colorists — learned the rules of the canon in training studios that fell under the authority of state institutions, temples, or local communities. These institutions provided instruction based on "pattern books" that yielded the secrets of artistic production. The trainees furnished the tools of their trade, and at the end of their apprenticeship, the best of them were kept on as government employees. These artistic technicians were managed by an "overseer of works," and they worked in teams of specialists, among whom men from a single family, more gifted than others, were often to be found. Their life was a privileged one: working on behalf of the eternity of important men, they rubbed shoulders with them and could even join their ranks. Anonymity and modesty were the rule for these people, as much as for the authors of the literary works that have come down to us: the notion of an artist's signature seems to have been entirely unknown to the Egyptian mentality. At the very most, an art historian of the present day is able to identify the work of a particular studio, but such attributions can only be made by the expert eye of a scholar.

The only individual talent to be recognized, and even cited as an example to pupils, was Imhotep, the genius who created stone architecture in Egypt, the inspired mind who conceived the pyramid of Djoser at Saqqara (c. 2700 B.C.E.). From the Middle Kingdom, only the artist Irtysen has gained notoriety, and not for his reputation as a good draftsman but rather from the fact that his son admired him so much that he erected a stela boasting of his father's talents. In its text Irtysen is presented as saying: "I know how to render the movement of a man who goes, as well as of a woman who comes, the bearing of a bird caught in a trap, the enthusiasm of one who clubs a lone prisoner, when his eye regards the one opposite him and the face of the enemy is distorted by fear; (I know how to render) the lifting of the arm of one who kills a hippopotamus, as well as the gait of one who runs."

THE TECHNIQUES OF RELIEF SCULPTURE

The most important task falling to the artists' studios was the preparation and carving of the reliefs on the walls of temples and tombs. What remains of them, still to be seen on site or in museums, affords a glimpse into the ongoing activity of these workplaces everywhere in the valley. Knowing that the cemeteries of Giza and Saqqara preserve hundreds of decorated mastabas from the Fourth to the Sixth Dynasties (2625–2200 B.C.E.), we can easily imagine the bustle and noise that reigned in the studios of the stonecutters and sculptors, and we can only regret that no important archaeological site has conserved any trace of them on its grounds.

The first team setting to work on the smooth surface of the dressed wall was that of the draftsmen, the "outline scribes." It was they who gave form to a scene, sketching in ink the lines and curves that would shape the bodies of the persons represented. Beginning with the Middle Kingdom, they drew a preliminary grid on the wall as a background to afford them guidelines for proportions and enable them to draw more accurately on the first try. Next came the team of sculptors, who would carve the relief with their copper chisels. They had at their disposal two techniques, which they chose according to the light the wall would receive or its location in the monument. The first technique was bas-relief, or raised relief, the cutting away of all the surface around the figures, who would remain in relief, their thickness projecting some inches from the hollowed-out background of the wall. The other technique was sunk relief, whereby only the surface within the figures was cut away, with levels cut back to create modeling and allow the play of light. Taken to its extreme, this technique became a sunken engraving in the hieroglyphic texts annotating the scenes, the interior surfaces of the signs being simply removed and leveled.

THE PAINTERS

Next arrived the painters, with their palettes, their broad brushes, and their narrow brushes made of reed stalks, whose ends they frayed by chewing them. They painted in tempera, spreading their paint in large, flat areas, without shadows or contours. Their palette was composed of six to eight cups, offering them a choice of colors to which tradition gradually assigned symbolic meanings. Yellow ocher was reserved for the skin of women; brown ocher distinguished the complexion of men; red was the color of violence and the forces of evil; blue, the attribute of the sky and the night; and green was the sign of youth and renewal. The powders of the colors were obtained from the ochers of the mountainside for yellow and red, from copper silicate for blue; the latter, mixed with yellow, made green. White was extracted from chalk, black drawn from charcoal. These pigments were diluted with water in a shell or a potsherd before being mixed with gum arabic or egg white, rendering them smooth and ready for application. These colors easily mixed, producing infinitely varied and shaded nuances, sometimes lively and sometimes deliberately drab. But in the age of the pyramids, however refined the technique might have been, painting was used only to set off the art of reliefs and statuary.

THE SCULPTORS

Even more so than in the case of bas-relief or drawing, the artist-artisan who produced statues was convinced he was creating a figure capable of coming to life. This idea is well expressed in the Egyptian vocabulary, which calls the sculptor a "fashioner of life" and a "modeler of forms" that an appropriate ritual could endow with life-giving breath; for the statue was intended to follow its subject into the afterlife as its exact double. To make "body and soul," as it were, correspond entirely, to make the finished statue correspond with the person it represented, a priest performed the "opening of the mouth" ritual on it, thus endowing it with the five vital senses. The person's name and titles were inscribed on the base or the back pillar of the statue to complete the process of bringing it to life and endowing it with an identity; this hieroglyphic label definitively verified the correspondence between the fleshly creature and the one made of stone, so that the two were forever merged. Statues of private people were potential repositories for the spiritual components of the dead. Those of gods, intended for the temples, were the object of attentive care from the clergy: in the first millennium, texts of the Greco-Roman Period relate that the priests washed and dressed them, fed them, and put them to bed, as though they were flesh and blood. As for the statues of kings, which were quite numerous from the Old Kingdom on, they had multiple functions: to accompany the sovereign in his afterlife and to serve as his representatives in the temples, in the company of his mythical fathers, the gods.

All the sculptors' studios applied the immutable laws of statuary to their products, endowing Egyptian statues with a distinctive style. Seated persons were represented frontally, with their heads set vertically on their shoulders, their impassive gaze fixed straight ahead of them, and their hands resting flat on their legs. Group statues, whether of a couple or a family, often give a strange impression; for each member of the group is represented sitting or standing upright, facing the viewer, no physical link, such as a glance or a slight tilt of the head, conveying the feelings that unite them. If, however, we look more closely, we can see the arm of the man, disproportionately long, placed tenderly around the waist of his wife. The statue of a standing deity or person would always represent its subject with the left foot for-

FIGURE 12.
Block statue of Seneb. Walters Art Gallery 22.166. Photo courtesy of The Walters Art Gallery, Baltimore.

ward. Beginning with the Middle Kingdom, "block statues" (Figure 12) were in fashion among the dignitaries. They form a unique category of Egyptian statuary, giving the impression that the man represented is one with the geometric cube of stone in which he is fashioned and from which only his head emerges. He is seated on the ground with his legs raised in front of him, his arms crossed, and his hands resting flat on his knees, the whole forming a compact mass. An ample robe envelops the person, hiding his body, which is scarcely distinguishable under the hieroglyphs carved in every direction all over the statue.

The representation of sculptors' workshops was a common theme on the walls of Old Kingdom mastabas. There we see the sculptors, often working in pairs, first rough-hewing the shape of the statue by striking the stone with blows from dolerite rollers or from stone hammers fitted into wooden tongs. Then they defined the contours of the object with copper chisels, which they guided with their hammers. The final appearance was achieved with the help of an adz, then a general rubbing with abrasive powder strewn on a round stone that served as a polisher. The statue passed next into the hands of the painters, who brought it to life with their exhilarating colors. Unfortunately, scarcely any traces of paint remain on the statues from the time of the pyramids, except for those of limestone, whose porous surface better absorbed the colors. The seated scribe in the Louvre and the life-sized couple Rehotpe and Nofret in the Cairo Museum are the most beautiful examples, showing to what an extent the enhancement of paint could bestow impressive presence on a statue.

Statues were made of all kinds of material, such as wood, ivory, copper, and bronze. But it was stone that gave the sculptors the opportunity to display their extraordinary skill. Their master works are of diorite, quartzite, basalt, alabaster, granite, schist, and limestone.

STONE VESSELS

Next to these sculptors, in the same studios, stonecutters specializing in the production of stone vessels busied themselves. Stone vessels were much sought after, for they signified wealth and luxury: their conspicuous solidity made them a symbol of durability, and their beauty destined them to be objects dedicated to eternity, gifts to accompany the deceased on the final journey. Cosmetics, perfumes, and oils were kept in them, and also fruits and grains. The tool used for drilling the stone was the very drill that designated an artisan in the hieroglyphs. It was composed of a wooden shaft surmounted by a crank and provided with a large bit that the stonecutter rotated to obtain the proper hollowing for his vase, jug, pot, or dish. Then he hewed the exterior with a hammer and polished it all with sand. The materials used for these vessels were hard stones extracted from the desert mountains: diorite, calcite, granite, porphyry, and breccia. The most beautiful stone vessels date from the fourth millennium, some centuries before the pyramids. Cut from basalt with flint tools, they display wonderfully pure, tapered shapes denoting total mastery of this craft.

CARPENTERS

Carpentry was always a major activity, as necessary for everyday affairs as for tomb furnishings. The guild of artisans who worked with wood, including all the specialists (woodworkers, cabinetmakers, carpenters, boatmakers), also played an important role in Egyptian society, which was pleased to have their many activities represented on the walls of their tombs. Local woods were unfortunately rare and of indifferent quality, offering poor opportunities for the artisans. Most of the time, they had to make do, choosing palm for carpentry; acacia for boats, coffins, tenons, and mortises; sycamore for statues, tables, and boxes; and tamarisk for small objects of daily use. Imported wood was more precious still, and it was reserved for the pharaoh and his court and for sacred furniture. Egyptians traveled into the heart of Africa in search of ebony, which lent itself so well to the modeling of harps and game boxes, and they sent expeditions to the Lebanon to furnish themselves with cedar, a hard wood perfectly suited for fashioning of the hulls of large boats.

Their tools were simple but permitted flawless production: axes, saws, adzes, chisels with wooden handles and blades of copper or bronze, awls to punch holes for drilling, bent drills to make the holes for tenons, and rollers covered with abrasive powder for the final polishing. The components of a piece were sometimes held together with vegetal glue, a pot of which was always kept warm in a corner of the workshop. Wooden rulers have been found in the tombs of artisans who wanted to take a valuable tool along into the afterlife, and thanks to their discovery, we know the pharaonic unit of measure: it was the "cubit" of 20.614 inches, that is, the length separating the elbow from the end of the middle finger. The cubit was divided into four "palms," which in turn were subdivided into four "fingers."

Like the sculptors, the craftsmen who worked with wood were assimilated into the ranks of the civil servants, and they functioned in teams distributed among the workshops managed by the royal palace, the temples, or the local communities. We see them at work in scenes from mastabas, fashioning coffins, scepters, temple kiosks, small columns, doors, latches, and

FIGURE 13.

Goats browsing a tree. From an Old Kingdom mastaba at Zawyet el-Maiyitin.
After C. R. Lepsius, Denkmaeler aus Aegypten und Aethiopien *(Berlin: Nicolai,*
1849–56), Part 2, Plate 108.

especially furniture: beds, stools, chairs, tables, cases, boxes, and chests.
Hieroglyphic inscriptions annotate their activities — "polishing a bed of
ebony by the polisher of the estate," "boring a case by a woodworker" —
or convey the partners' dialogues: "Take another saw, comrade, this one is
hot," or, quite often, "Watch out for your fingers!"

THE SHIPYARD

The building of a ship was the most important commission a workshop
could receive, entailing the construction of a boat, for public or ritual transport, that was more efficient than the papyrus crafts used for everyday
transportation. Around 2625 B.C.E., Snofru ordered the "construction of a
boat of 100 cubits (called) 'Adoration of the Two Lands' of cedar wood and
two other boats of 100 cubits." Reliefs in mastabas depict the setting of a
shipyard located near a plantation of acacias, where the trees chosen by the
woodcutters were turned over, still standing, to the goats, which browsed
their leaves, baring the trunks and the main branches (Figure 13). Later the
woodcutters returned and felled the trees, cut up the trunks, removed the
knots, and then split the wood with blows of axes and adzes. The joiners
took this wood and prepared the planks of the hull they were assembling
with the help of mortises and large tenons. "Fitting the bulwark" and "fitting the ship's rail" are frequent annotations to these scenes, in the course
of which the men cry out, "Come right down," and "I'll crush your hands!
Watch out for us!" This joinery, followed by an application of adhesive
resin to fill in the last gaps, guaranteed the watertightness of the ship. The

workmen polished their boat with infinite care, and finally they attached a light, mobile cabin to it. At the end of their work, one of them could at last exclaim, "I'm going to see something beautiful!"

GOLDSMITHS AND BLACKSMITHS

Metalworkers also worked in teams and in workshops. To be sure, there was a hierarchy and a genuine class difference between the hapless copper-smith in the street, described by the "Satire of the Trades" as one "whose fingers are like crocodile scales and who stinks more than fish eggs," and the goldsmith in the royal studios fashioning the adornments of the great. The former busied themselves with working the copper imported from the eastern desert and Sinai; the latter wrought gold and electrum, precious metals obtained in the desert of Nubia. The reliefs from the causeway of the pyramid of Wenis at Saqqara give a good idea of what a smithy was like in the Old Kingdom. First came the delivery and weighing of the ingots, under the supervision of the "inspector of metalworkers" or the "inspector of scales." The ingots sometimes arrived at the studio still covered with dirt and could cause an unpleasant surprise at the weighing: above one scene, we read, "That's not an ingot, it's a stone!" The real ingots passed into the hands of the smelters, who placed the cleaned metal in a crucible suspended above a fire, which they stoked by blowing vigorously through two reed tubes. The crucible was pierced on one side, and as the metal melted, it flowed out through this opening. The manufacture of metal objects was accomplished by cold-hammering and beating the metal with stone hammers. The pieces of metal were bent, placed in molds, riveted together, and finally sanded to remove all traces of joints. The objects most frequently produced were weapons, tools, and funerary vessels: plates, dishes, bowls, and pitchers.

The goldsmiths' studios received their gold, called "flesh of the gods" in religious texts, in the form of dust, which they melted in small crucibles heated to more than 1,800° F. Once cooled and hardened, the gold was converted into thin sheets that were roughly shaped by hammering. This gold foil was then used to cover wooden cult objects and divine statues and even nailed onto the doors of temples. Jewelers' work displays a total mastery of the techniques of incising and enameling. Gold jewelry was enhanced by inlays of semiprecious stones (carnelian, lapis lazuli, turquoise), faience, and rock crystal. In the Old Kingdom, the manufacture of large, beaded collars called *usekh* seems to have been the specialty of dwarf jew-

elers. Indeed, though the annotations to the scenes do not tell us why, we often see two very small men on either side of a table, at work stringing beads or knotting the strings (Figure 14). Once finished, they dipped their collar into an unidentified liquid that lent it brilliance and hardness by any test.

CERAMIC WORKSHOPS

Potters acquired their raw material without difficulty: they had only to bend down on the banks of the Nile to collect the clay for their ceramics. After trampling and kneading it, they mixed it with water, cow dung, and straw to achieve the smooth paste they modeled on their wheel (Figure 15), a device known in Egypt since the earliest dynasties. With this method, from the outset, a considerable diversity of wares issued from the expert hands of the potters: bowls, dishes, plates, cups, goblets, pots, terrines, tumblers, vases, jars, and carafes entered the kitchens to become a part of everyday life. This earthenware was fired in kilns and finished cold. Its exterior surface was covered with a reddish, liquid slip that gave it a polished, ruddy appearance. For decoration, a stylus or a comb could be used to incise dots or geometric lines, and the piece could be completed with figurative designs in black or white paint.

At the Sixth Dynasty town site of Balat (c. 2300 B.C.E.) in el-Dakhla Oasis, archaeologists discovered a zone of pottery workshops, with an area for preparing the clay in basins, a wing reserved for firing with its kilns still in place, and a sector for drying and finishing. The potters did not have the best lot among artisans; their working conditions were harsh, like those of the brewers and bakers at whose side they are regularly shown working in

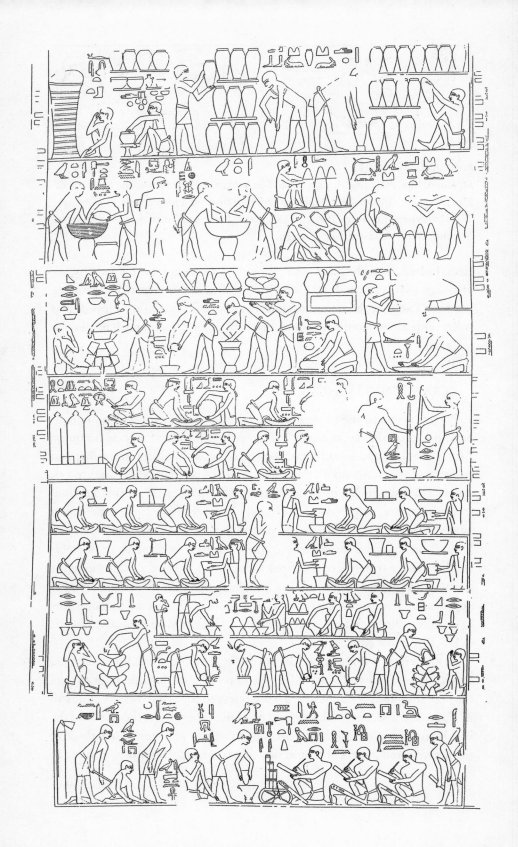

the tomb paintings of the Middle Kingdom. Their status accorded them no privileges, undoubtedly because their work was purely utilitarian and their output not destined for the furnishings of tombs. Disparaging manual labor so as to exalt the scribal profession, the author of the "Satire of the Trades," Khety, speaks thus of the potter: "(He) lives 'under ground,' while still among the living. He uproots his plants, trampling in the mud more than a pig to warm his pots. His clothes are stiff with clay, his girdle is in tatters."

TANNERS AND COBBLERS

As early as the prehistoric period, leatherwork was well known in Egypt. In the mastabas, numerous reliefs show tanners and sandal makers pulling on their animal skins or applying oil and alum to make a supple, waterproof material for sacks, cases, drinking skins, bellows for the fire, and sandals. In the Old Kingdom, Uta, manager of a royal workshop devoted to all sorts of leatherwork, noted in his titles the manufactured items for which he was responsible: "The overseer of the tanning of royal manuscript cases, chief of secrets, he who satisfies the heart of his lord in works of tanning, Uta. The overseer of the tanning of the royal sandals . . . , the overseer of the artisans of parchment, who caused the parchment rolls of the lector priest to be made according to the wishes of his master, in conformity with what had been commanded." The air of the tanneries was unbreathable because of the odor emanating from the animal skins. Again, the "Satire of the Trades" says of the cobbler, "He feels as good as one would feel among corpses, and what he bites is leather."

SPINNING AND WEAVING: A WOMEN'S TRADE

In the time of the pyramids, spinning and weaving were the work of women, who thus cornered an exclusively female professional activity, one that was recognized and carried out in workshops, with specialties and the

FIGURE 15.
Ceramic workshop. From the Old Kingdom mastaba of Ty at Saqqara. After Lucienne Épron, François Daumas, Georges Goyon, and Pierre Montet, Le Tombeau de Ti, *Mémoirs publiés par les membres de l'Institut Français d'Archéologie Orientale du Caire 65, fascicle 1 (Cairo: Institut Français d'Archéologie Orientale du Caire: 1939), Plate LXVI. © IFAO. Reproduced by permission of the Institut Français d'Archéologie Orientale du Caire.*

FIGURE 16.

Wooden model of a weavers' studio. From the Middle Kingdom tomb of Meketre at Thebes. Cairo Museum JE 46729. Photo courtesy of The Louvre.

customary hierarchy. In exchange for their production, the weavers received goods in kind or, as vanity obliged, jewelry. A wooden model from the tomb of Meketre (c. 2000 B.C.E.; Figure 16) and a painting from the tomb of Khnumhotpe (c. 1950) at Beni Hasan illustrate the operation of these shops, which were run by a "directress of weavers": seated on the ground, the spinsters twist their flaxen fibers and wind their threads into balls, which they then spin on wooden spindles. Beside them, two women busy themselves around a loom, raising the rows of warp thread, while two others pass a shuttle back and forth to make the weft, which they periodically press tight with a wooden reed. Once finished, the pieces of cloth were marked with ink, thus carrying the label of the studio from which they came, markings especially precious to the archaeologist discovering them several millennia later. Until the end of the Middle Kingdom, looms were horizontal and placed on the ground, so that the women were obliged to work stooped over or sitting on the floor. It was not until the New Kingdom that the vertical loom appeared and the male sex gradually replaced women in the workshops.

BASKETMAKING

Often discovered today in an excellent state of preservation, objects of basketry were of service to all in their everyday life and accompanied the most humble in their afterlife. Just as today, mats woven from reeds or straw enabled people to sit in a group under a tree without fear of insects, to stretch out to sleep, or to settle themselves on benches in front of their houses to chat with neighbors at sunset. Basketry was also used in the burials of the poor: in humble cemeteries unembellished by stone construction of any size, Egyptians have been found buried directly in pits, rolled up in rush mats that were both their coffins and their tombs.

The making of basketwork objects seems always to have been a part of women's daily work at home; Egyptian society apparently never felt the need to make it an activity of specific workshops. Baskets and trays were spiral woven from palm fronds, as is still done by Nubians. Sacks made of bundles of cords fastened to one another have been discovered filled with grain; they were used by women who went off with their husbands to the fields, sack slung over shoulder, to do the sowing.

The permanence of the forms and techniques of basketwork, from the very dawn of history on, is one of the most striking features of Egyptian craft industries. In fact it is often difficult to believe that millennia separate the baskets on display in the cases of museums from their counterparts offered today by merchants in the *souk*s of Luxor and Aswan.

6 FAMILY LIFE

To teach them their profession and instill a code of ethics, young scribes were made to copy numerous wisdom texts. These all insist on the necessity of taking a wife and founding a household, presenting married life as the secret to happiness and the guarantee of successful integration into society. "If you prosper, found a household, take a wife, and cherish her in your house, as is proper. Fill her belly, clothe her back. . . . Keep her happy so long as you live. She is a fertile field for her lord. . . . If you take a wife who is joyful, if every moment has its attractions for her, do not reject her, nourish her well" — so we read in the maxims attributed to Ptahhotpe, the vizier of Djedkare Izezi of the Fifth Dynasty and the presumed author of the first known treatise on ethics in the history of humankind.

FOUNDING A HOUSEHOLD

For a young man, marriage age was when his material and professional circumstances permitted him to provide for the needs of a family. Again, Ptahhotpe advises his young readers, "If you have already made a name, you can found a household." It seems to have been accepted that a young man could enjoy the pleasures of the single life at the end of his adolescence, whereas an Egyptian girl married at a younger age, often at the onset of puberty, around twelve or thirteen. Such an early age can seem shocking today, though it is still the practice in certain countries of black Africa. It must be remembered, moreover, that in rural areas, the average life expectancy was thirty years, which had the effect of lowering the age of entry into adult life to below that of fifteen.

The Egyptian vocabulary had no term corresponding to our word *engagement,* or even our word *marriage,* but it had two distinct terms for *woman* — one for a person of the female gender, the other for "wife." In biographical inscriptions, men relate that they were married through roundabout expressions such as "to take a wife" and "to found a household." But there is no indication that a civil or religious ceremony consecrated the union of the spouses: marriage was a private act, without a legal framework, given concrete expression by the "founding of the household" and the ensuing cohabitation of the spouses. Nor is there any trace of a marriage contract in the time of the pyramids; this type of document is not to be found until the first millennium B.C.E.

It was the father of the girl who chose the future husband and gave his consent to the marriage, after discussions and negotiations with the family of the young man. Whether among the rich or the peasants, marriage seems to have been arranged by the families of the two parties, the girl being at the disposal of her father and obliged to comply with his interests. On a wall of his tomb, the nobleman Ptahshepses declares, "His Majesty gave him his eldest daughter . . . as wife, because his Majesty desired that she be with him rather than any other man."

Nevertheless, fathers — or at least some of them — took the aspirations of their daughters into account. Love is not absent from representations of couples or from the literature. Quite often, statues show a man and his wife tenderly embracing while their children sit at their feet, affectionately clinging to their legs. On the walls of mastabas, the owner often has his wife represented at his side, associating the two with the happy moments they spent on earth and naming them with love.

A man chose his future wife in the near family or in the very bosom of his town. It is probable that marriages between cousins were frequent, as is still the case in modern Egypt. But the Egyptian vocabulary is extremely poor in terms distinguishing the kinds and degrees of kinship that we habitually establish in genealogical research. Moreover, homonymy makes our task more difficult. Often, in a single family, whose names we can read on a collective funerary stela, the men all have the same name and occupation: how then are we to know whether a sister married her brother, her cousin, or even a neighbor who had the same name? We find a certain number of marriages between paternal uncles and their nieces and between paternal aunts and their nephews. Marriage between brother and sister seems to have been reserved for the royal family, to maintain its cohesion. This consanguinity stopped there: in the age of the pyramids, there is no example of a pharaoh marrying his daughter.

MIXED MARRIAGES AND POLYGAMY

Men thus tended to find their mates in their immediate surroundings. A certain distrust of "mixed" marriages appears in the advice lavished on young men by the authors of the wisdom literature: "Beware of a woman who is unknown in your town. Do not look at her as though she were better than others; do not know her sexually: she is like a deep water whose eddy is not known," the sage Any would write at the beginning of the New Kingdom (c. 1550 B.C.E.). Nevertheless, the fortunes of life led some Egyptians to marry a foreigner: thus Sinuhe, the hero of a popular novel, married an Asiatic princess and founded his household in his land of exile. But at the end of the story, when at last he was able to return to his beloved land of Egypt, he left his wife and children behind, fearing no doubt that these "foreigners" would not easily adapt to Egyptian customs.

Polygamy was not forbidden but apparently was seldom practiced. In fact, from earliest times on, the nuclear family of two adults and their children seems to have been the basis of domestic life, and this practice remained the custom in the Christian period, scarcely changing until the coming of Islam to Egypt in the eighth century of our own era. The texts distinguish, however, between wives and concubines, insisting on the privileged status of the legitimate wife. A concubine was sheltered under the roof of the master of the house and could have children by him, but she was subject to his good will and could be summarily expelled when she ceased to please. Her children could be adopted by their father. The legitimate wife owed obedience and fidelity to her husband; a single indiscretion on her part would imperil the family honor. One of the literary tales recorded on Papyrus Westcar shows to what extent infidelity bore the stamp of opprobrium. This account is set in the reign of King Nebka, a predecessor of Khephren, and depicts a magician-priest, his wife, and her lover, who is called a "commoner." After several attempts at seduction, the amorous frolics of the lovers took place in a garden pavilion, where "they spent a happy day," a time-honored expression for carnal pleasure. But the gardener was watching and denounced the couple to his master. The latter, like a good magician, then made a wax crocodile that was miraculously transformed into a gigantic, live crocodile seven cubits (about twelve feet) long, which devoured the "commoner." As for the wife, the pharaoh himself saw to her punishment: "She was taken to a field north of the royal Residence. He had her burned, and her ashes were scattered in the Nile."

A special society, very different from that of the common people, developed at the royal court. There, polygamy was practically obligatory: the harem was a royal institution in which a group of women were ruled by a codified hierarchy. At its head reigned the "great royal wife," the one to be found at the king's side at royal appearances. But the harem was not there solely to satisfy the diverse fantasies of the pharaoh: rather, it was an instrument of pharaonic power, one which, through the play of extensive alliances, consolidated the great political forces of the country and secured the good will of neighboring lands.

DIVORCE

Among private people, divorce was permitted when the adultery, infidelity, or sterility of the wife was established. As in marriage, no text governed the conventions of divorce; it was a matter of repudiation pure and simple, needing no judicial or religious intervention. For the age of the pyramids, there is very little documentation mentioning marital breakups or conjugal dramas; rather, one is struck by the tenderness and depth of feeling expressed in representations of couples in this period.

Once married, the man and his wife took up residence in their house, which in principle was supposed to be supplied by the family of the young man, along with the fields and other material goods that would nourish the future household. The young woman, who had been instructed by her mother since childhood in the duties of a good housewife, took possession of her new domain. From the Old Kingdom on, in every text mentioning a married woman, her name was preceded by the title *nebet per*, "mistress of the house," the equivalent of our "Mrs.," specifying thus that the chief task of a wife was to take good care of her house and those it sheltered.

HAVING CHILDREN

From the first months of their marriage, the young couple aspired to have children, who would be the source of their happiness and social esteem, as well as their guarantee of descendants to assure their funerary cult. The love of parents for their children is expressed unselfconsciously in literature and in representations of families. Thus the "Story of the Shipwrecked Sailor" contains these words brimming with lofty sentiments: "You will clasp your children to your bosom, you will kiss your wife, you will see your home again, and that is better than anything." Parental love is also attested by infant burials in which the little bodies are treated with affection and piety.

The representation of pregnant women is frequent in female statuettes and figurines dating to Egyptian prehistory, but it disappeared at the same time that pharaonic civilization was born, as though a newfound modesty veiled this condition, albeit common, with discretion. Nevertheless, on a wall of the mastaba of Ankhmahor, royal architect of the pharaoh Teti (c. 2450 B.C.E.), buried at Saqqara, we note scenes of a funeral attended by some pregnant women. One of them faints, moreover, under the combined effect of her emotion and the heat.

Knowledge of sexual matters was rather limited. The Egyptians believed that sperm was secreted by the bones and that conception could occur through the mouth as well as the vagina. The latter is called "the mortar" in the Pyramid Texts; it is there that the life of the embryo was supposed to be fashioned. The nourishment of the baby in utero was provided by the mother's menstrual blood, diverted to the benefit of the infant during pregnancy. Expectant mothers had a whole arsenal of magico-medical practices at their disposal to avoid false labor, premature birth, or miscarriage, and their prayers went out to the protective deities of childbirth: the female hippopotamus Taweret, and Bes, the gnome who was the scourge of evil spirits. The formidable number of spells intended to protect pregnancy and birth shows that infant mortality and the death of women in labor were quite frequent, afflicting families with grief.

Childbirth took place at home and was the affair of professional wisewomen and of the other women of the family. The mother-to-be knelt or crouched over a platform composed of two bricks set wide apart, between which the child was supposed to appear. It was the wisewoman who supervised the labor, helped with the delivery, and gave the newborn its initial care. The umbilical cord was cut only when the infant had been washed and the placenta expelled. Several texts mention multiple births, which are estimated to have been a hundredth of total births. Infant mortality was increased tenfold by the complications caused by the arrival of twins, very few of whom survived. Nevertheless, two brothers who were apparently twins, Neankhkhnum and Khnumhotpe, became famous at the court of kings Neuserre and Menkauhor of the Fifth Dynasty (c. 2500 B.C.E.), sharing the office of overseer of palace manicurists. Even death did not separate them: they were buried together at Saqqara, in a vast tomb whose reliefs stress the special nature of their family ties.

To lend credence to the myth of the semidivine pharaoh, extraordinary manifestations had to accompany his birth, as signs of the miraculous nature of the event. One of the tales of Papyrus Westcar relates thus the legendary birth of the first kings of the Fifth Dynasty, whose tutelary father was Re: "One day, it happened that Ruddjedet felt the pangs of birth. Then the Majesty of Re . . . said to the deities Isis, Nephthys, Meskhenet, Heqet, and Khnum, 'Hasten, then, to deliver Ruddjedet of the three children who are in her womb and who will in the future exercise this illustrious and beneficent office in this entire land; they will build the temples of your cities, they will provision your altars.'" Like good fairies, the divinities hastened to the bedside of the royal mother to tend her until the first child appeared: "Then this child slipped into the hands (of Isis), a child one cubit long; his bones were hard, his limbs were covered with gold, his hair was of real lapis lazuli." Three royal children were thus born, made of gold and precious stone. Ruddjedet then spent fourteen days in the "birth tent," a shelter reserved for postnatal rest and "purification." Whether at the royal palace or in a peasant's farmhouse, a woman was considered impure and defiled by her blood after giving birth. It was necessary to wait for things to return to order for her to be permitted back under the family roof.

At birth, little Egyptians received a name that would remain with them throughout existence, like an inseparable part of their being. This name, which always had a meaning, could be related to the circumstances of the moment: "I am happy," "What satisfaction," "It is happy for me," "A son for me," "I will not give him up," or again, "He who comes bearing happiness." The conferring of the name could also reflect a quality observed or desired in the infant: "Bright," "Friend," "Beloved," "Clever," "Joyful," "Deaf," "Strong," "Weak." Parents sometimes wished to place their child under the protection of a deity and assigned it a theophoric name — "Horus," "Khons," "She who belongs to Mut" — or even recalled a great reign with a basilophoric name, such as "Snofru," "Inyotef," or "Amenemhet."

Despite a high rate of infant mortality (one death out of two or three births), the number of children per family remained high, reaching an average of four to six. Certain families, blessed with robust health from birth, could boast of ten or even fifteen children! Adoption is regularly mentioned beginning with the New Kingdom, and there is no reason to think it unknown in the age of the pyramids. The solution to a couple's sterility could be found in the adoption of the children the husband had by a concubine.

A retarded, handicapped, or deformed child was usually abandoned: it was considered a being marked by fate, rejected by the gods, for whom any hope was in vain, any effort useless.

NURSING, BOTTLE FEEDING, AND LAYETTE

The upbringing of a young child was entrusted to its mother, who nursed it until the age of three. For the child, this was a guarantee of suitable nourishment, and for her, a method of contraception whose effectiveness had been understood since earliest times. To nurse, the mother sat on the ground and held her little one on her knees, with no qualms about showing herself in public. Even Princess Sobeknakhte of the Twelfth Dynasty (c. 1950 B.C.E.) allowed herself to be represented in this manner in a bas-relief. A great many statuettes depict a woman holding her child to her breast, expressing in this way the very image of fecundity and a certain form of feminine ideal. Outdoors, the young mother had her baby astride her hip, holding it in a shawl that served as a baby carrier. She thus kept her hands free and could return to her activities, in the fields for example, shortly after giving birth.

One of the most widespread and highly respected female occupations was that of nurse. Among the well-to-do, it was common for a mother to entrust the nursing of her baby to a wet nurse whose job it was to care for the child until the age of three. In exchange for her milk and the care she committed herself to provide unstintingly, the nurse was housed and fed by the family, who could thus monitor the well-being of the child. For baby bottles, the Egyptians used baked-clay dishes with elongated spouts, some of which have been found in child burials.

The layette was kept to a minimum, if we are to believe the bas-reliefs and statues, where nudity stands out as the external sign of extreme youth (Figure 17). Children began to wear clothes at puberty; even so, it is not rare to see girls with their breasts already formed playing nude with their friends. One cannot help wondering, however, whether the nudity of children was instead an artistic convention facilitating immediate distinctions between younger and older children, when in reality, things were different. For winter evenings were sometimes quite cold, and we can hardly believe that Egyptian parents would have left their children without clothing. In the tomb of a girl of the Eleventh Dynasty (c. 2100 B.C.E.), discovered at Saqqara in 1982, archaeologists found the front of a little V-necked dress, tied at the neck with a string, which was intended to clothe the child in the afterlife. Here and there, excavations have uncovered the tatters of little

FIGURE 17.
Statue of Seneb and his family. Cairo Museum JE 51281. Photo by Costa. Photo courtesy of the Metropolitan Museum of Art.

articles of clothing, proving that children were not always as nude as the reliefs would have us believe.

THE SIDELOCK OF YOUTH

Hair was also a specific sign of childhood; in fact boys and girls wore a lock of hair on the right side of the head, the rest being shaved off or cut short. Moreover, in hieroglyphic texts, words pertaining to childhood are determined by this curled lock, and this hair style was also that of child-gods. For three thousand years, pharaonic Egypt would maintain a standard iconography of the child: it went nude, with its sidelock, and its finger in its mouth, indicating recent weaning. Its nudity did not rule out some jewelry — bracelets, necklaces, and various amulets worn as pendants to ward off the evil spirits who brought miasmas. The lock of hair was sometimes tied with a loop of string decorated with a jewel. Thus the daughter of the Twelfth Dynasty (c. 1950 B.C.E.) nomarch Wekh-hotpe of Meir in Middle Egypt took pains with her hair for a family outing, and her tress was tied with a jewel in the form of a fish, which could have been of turquoise, lapis lazuli, or carnelian, if we go by specimens preserved in museums today.

GAMES AND TOYS

As soon as children could walk, their mothers gladly let them play outdoors in front of the house with their siblings and their little neighbors. Toys were above all things picked up from the ground: pebbles became jacks, cloth was rolled into balls, and game boards were drawn on potsherds. Children's toys were discovered in the houses of the town of el-Lahun, which sheltered the men who worked on the pyramid of Senwosret II (1895–1878 B.C.E.). There, large and small balls were made of pieces of stitched leather stuffed with straw or dried barley; two-toned tops were of wood or faience. Dolls of wood or clay can also be regarded as toys; some even have arms with joints and removable wigs, and they must have afforded plenty of distraction for the little girls when the weather brought wind and sand! Animal figurines in the form of hippopotamuses, crocodiles, pigs, and monkeys populated the imaginary farms of the little Egyptians. These "toys" in the form of miniature animals have often been found at townsites, such as Balat and el-Lahun, where remains from the Old and Middle Kingdoms have been preserved. While they were young, boys and girls played together, as attested by a little sculpture group from the Old Kingdom showing two children of the opposite sex playing leapfrog.

To amuse themselves, children on the banks of the Nile could also turn to their domestic animals. Before the cat, which did not appear until the New Kingdom (c. 1550 B.C.E.), pigeons, hoopoes, and dogs were the chosen companions of children in the Egyptian countryside. These animals were rarely leashed; they walked freely beside their young masters, who gave them affectionate names. Dogs followed the members of the household on their hunting and fishing excursions, which are described as the happiest times of relaxation and enjoyment for all the members of the family.

As the children grew up, their games resembled physical exercises, such as acrobatic contests in which the young men would display their strength and virility. The grape harvest occasioned a ritualized game called "shooting for Shezemu," the god of the wine press. The rules required the children to throw darts at targets placed on the ground. One boys' game known from several representations seems brutal, almost cruel: one of the adolescents was captured by a group of youths and cornered in an enclosed area. Like a mouse trapped by a cat, he had to escape from this tight spot on his own. If he succeeded, he was considered "great." The little girls did not take part in this sort of exercise; they studied dancing, practicing to take part in the festivals honoring the goddess Hathor, mistress of music, love, and dance.

EDUCATION AND TRANSITION TO ADULTHOOD

For boys in the time of the pyramids, the transition to adulthood was marked by circumcision, a regular practice in the third millennium, though it seems to have been less widespread later. A scene from the mastaba of Ankhmahor at Saqqara (c. 2450 B.C.E.) shows the unfolding of this quasi-ritual act. An adolescent of about twelve or thirteen is led before an assistant, who dabs his penis with a product intended to ease the pain to come. Then he is held standing and immobilized by another assistant, while the priest-surgeon quickly conducts the operation, saying to his aide, "Hold him firmly, don't let him faint." It seems, moreover, that Egyptian circumcision entailed a simple incision of the foreskin, not its entire removal. Other texts speak of a group ceremony, as though all young men of age in the town underwent this ritual act at the same time. A notable who lived around 2100 B.C.E. relates, "When I was circumcised, at the same time as one hundred twenty others, none of us was wounded or torn." As for girls, the texts make no mention of clitoridectomy; examination of the mummies of women confirms that it was not practiced.

So, blessed with several children, Egyptian families lived in their simple houses of unbaked brick and inculcated in their offspring the principles of a solid upbringing. The father took it upon himself to turn his sons into good little Egyptians, beginning by setting an example of one happy to have adhered since childhood to the moral and social order of his land. The basic principles of Egyptian society lay in obedience to and respect for an equilibrium granted by the gods but incessantly threatened by the forces of Evil. To maintain this equilibrium, each individual had to adapt to the group and carry on the traditions of the ancients. The education of children had a double mission: to guide them in respecting the mores of society and, little by little, to teach them the practice of their future profession, which in all likelihood would be that of their father.

As early as the Old Kingdom, the maxims of the sage Ptahhotpe reveal the secrets of a successful education: "If you are a man of worth, and if you have had a son by the grace of the god, if he is proper, if he is similar to your nature, if he listens to your instructions. . . . If he takes care of your possessions . . . , then seek to do good for him, for he is your son. . . . Do not separate your heart from his." This same Ptahhotpe who advises young men to found a household and watch over their wives gives stern warning against the attractions of homosexuality and pedophilia: "Do not copulate with an effeminate boy . . . do not allow him to spend the night doing what is forbidden; . . . thus he will be calm after staving off his desire." In one literary tale, homosexuality is presented as ridiculous behavior, the more so as it is attributed to a pharaoh suspected of maintaining a special friendship with the head of his army. This was a basic violation of Egyptian morality and of the code regulating the good conduct one had the right to expect of everyone and, a fortiori, of the highest personage in the state.

FROM HOUSE TO CITY: SETTLEMENTS

Our knowledge of cities, towns, and houses in the Old and Middle Kingdoms is limited to rare traces of domestic architecture identified at townsites. These last, unfortunately, are for the most part destroyed or covered by more recent construction. As a general rule, the Egyptians founded their towns on elevated sites safe from the inundation, a rule observed until the 1960s when the construction of the High Dam at Aswan put an end to the annual Nile flood. To uncover the remains of ancient habitations whose basic material was fragile, unbaked bricks, archaeologists must destroy many strata of later constructions in the slim hope of reaching a period as remote in time as the one in which they are interested. By chance, some town sites had a brief life span, their locations having been chosen more for political reasons than because they were well situated with regard to the inundation. This was the case with certain sites in areas now desert, such as Ain-Asil or el-Lahun, which were occupied only briefly.

Extending over nearly one hundred acres, Ain-Asil shelters the remains of the regional capital founded by the governors of el-Dakhla Oasis, in the western desert, at the end of the Old Kingdom (between about 2400 and 2100 B.C.E.). Excavations by the French Institute of Oriental Archaeology have shown that this city developed within large enclosure walls, fortified with towers, which surrounded dwellings and areas of activity. Well-preserved traces can be observed there of administrative, military, and religious buildings, the last including the funerary chapels of the governors, whose bodies were buried several hundred yards away in the huge mastabas of the cemetery of Balat. Small dwellings are rather difficult to find: all the buildings are spacious, with certain houses having an area of as much as nearly two hundred square feet, with a place for cooking and baking, and bedrooms arranged around a courtyard.

The layout of the town of el-Lahun, in the province of the Faiyum, is rather different. This town was founded by Senwosret II (1881–1873 B.C.E.), when the pharaohs of the Middle Kingdom moved the administrative center of the country from Memphis to the Faiyum, at the junction of Upper and Lower Egypt, for better supervision of all the land. They also had their pyramids erected there: the function of the town of el-Lahun was to house, along with their families, the managers and workmen who built the pyramid of Senwosret II. Its population has been estimated at about five thousand people. The town is delimited by a thick enclosure wall forming a rectangle about 440 yards long by 380 yards wide. Inside, two sectors can be clearly distinguished, corresponding to two well-differentiated social classes. In the east, the side of the notables and courtiers, a dozen homes display a spacious plan (between 11,000 square feet and 26,000 square feet); they are well ventilated and organized around a peristyle court that led to several reception rooms. There is direct access from the street to the kitchens, the lodgings of the staff, and the cellars. In the part of the "villa" that housed the owner and his family, a long corridor leads to the owner's suite and to enough bedrooms to accommodate more than fifty people. Certain of these were provided with bathrooms, whose walls were lined with stone slabs coated with plaster. The floor was paved, and water, once used, ran into a receptacle built into the ground, which the household staff would empty regularly. House walls were always of unbaked bricks, which were made by mixing straw and mud and then placing this cob into wooden molds to dry in the sun. They were constructed with the help of a mortar of straw, mud, and sand, with which the mason coated each wall when it was raised. Wooden columns supported the roof, whose beams were half trunks of palm trees covered with palm leaves, matting, or bundles of reeds or papyrus, all held together by a layer of cob applied with a gentle slope toward the exterior to facilitate the runoff of water in the event of rain. A stairway made it possible to go up to the rooftop terrace, which afforded a place for relaxation at sunset, when one wished to take advantage of the evening air. Openings were generally on the north, from which there blew a soothing and refreshing breeze. To keep the interior of the house cool, the windows, which were set in the upper part of the walls, were narrow and let in only what light and air were needed. There were no openings on the west, so as to protect against the violent, choking sandstorms that blew from the Sahara, invading the sky every spring. The doors, which were made of wood, pivoted on hinges set into the threshold and lintel, and they were closed with latches. The floors were of beaten earth; the thresholds and lintels were often carved from stone.

On the west side stretched the workmen's village, two hundred dwellings squeezed against one another and rarely having more than three rooms — a reception room, one or two bedrooms, and a kitchen containing a hearth for baking bread, a millstone, and a silo — all was surmounted by a rooftop terrace. In the west as in the east, and as in all the archaeological remains of townsites of this era, the principles and techniques of construction scarcely varied: unbaked brick and mortar would remain the basic material for all domestic architecture in pharaonic Egypt. They are still to be found in the villages of modern Upper Egypt, and the study of present-day dwellings is of undeniable help to the archaeologist attempting to set the Egyptians from the time of the pyramids in the framework of their everyday lives.

DAILY LIFE

Getting rid of the household garbage, battling rodents, and fetching water were the daily concerns of Egyptian households. There were no sanitation facilities; the nearest canal usually received the garbage, when it was not simply heaped up in a dump outside the town. At el-Lahun, archaeologists have identified a garbage dump outside the enclosure wall. Flies and mosquitoes swarmed, especially in the swampy delta. The Greek historian Herodotus even recounts that the inhabitants of the delta, which he visited in the fifth century B.C.E., used their fishing nets as mosquito nets to get a peaceful night's sleep. Fleas and other bugs shamelessly invaded the animals and furniture in the homes, while the granaries and kitchens were irresistible attractions for rats and mice no cat would threaten, for the cat had not yet been domesticated.

The responsibility of providing water for each household and for the government offices was assumed at the local level. The women went to the canal in groups, as the sun set in the evening, and brought their heavy jars filled with water, carefully balanced on their heads, back to town. Personal hygiene, doing the dishes, washing clothes, and housecleaning consumed considerable water, and the women had to make frequent trips. Large-scale laundering seems, however, to have been a job for men, who went to the Nile or the canal and did their wash on the spot, while their youngest children bathed under their watchful eyes. Construction sites and brickyards had recourse to professional water carriers, who sometimes used donkeys to carry their burden.

Ancient towns were thus composed of modest houses squeezed together along narrow alleys, swarming with a boisterous and joyful population. The lighting of these homes with their narrow apertures was provided by lamps, of which numerous examples have been found; they are little stone or baked-clay cups, in which twisted wicks coated with oil were burned. Except at the royal court, furniture was modest — composed mainly of wooden chests in which the household pottery and linens were put away. Seats were simple cubic stools; pedestal tables could hold pottery or a meal in progress. The floor was strewn with mats on which people slept; for beds made of wood were reserved for the well-to-do. There were nighttime bedheads; for these uncomfortable-looking headrests of wood or stone were meant to promote sleep and protect people from the stings of crawling insects.

Along the interior and exterior walls, benches made of unbaked brick enabled people to sit, receiving neighbors and friends, and also to sleep. This feature, perfectly integrated into the architecture of the house, is still to be seen in the villages of Upper Egypt and the oases of the western desert. These benches are the most tangible, and also the most pleasant, mark of the social and domestic workings characteristic of the life style of the Egyptians, for whom welcoming friends and getting their rest have always been definite priorities.

7   A BUSY DAY

Ptahhotpe, vizier and minister of justice around 2400 B.C.E., was an exception among the Egyptians: he was practically the only one to have himself represented getting up in the early morning. Thanks to him, we can imagine the beginning of a day on the banks of the Nile, keeping in mind that the scene unfolds in the home of a vizier, the second-ranking personage of the state. Upon awakening, Ptahhotpe readies himself to have his servants attend to his grooming. The domestic staff is numerous; it takes no fewer than six servants to present the master with his clothing for the day, shave him, do his hair, polish his fingernails, and wash his feet. At Pharaoh's court, we find a high-ranking personage, the "director of the king's toilette," whose job was supervising the large staff occupied with caring for his majesty's body. The king needed to feel clean and freshly shaven at all times.

Among more ordinary folk, shaving was a job for the barber, who dealt with hair and beard at the same time. The scene took place outdoors, with the barber seated on a stool at the right height to shave the customer squatting at his feet. In the third millennium, a razor was a simple blade of stone, with one edge well sharpened, fitted into a wooden handle. But we already find some examples of copper and bronze blades, which would subsequently become the common shaving tools.

Heat, dust, and work in the fields led to a frequent desire to freshen up, and daily washing was a necessity. Most often, people made do with washing their face and hands, dipping them in a bowl of water poured from a jar. On bath days, they soaked in plenty of water in something like a modern tub. Bathing and removal of body hair are mentioned as a ritual obligation for temple personnel.

CLOTHING

Weaving and making clothes were exclusively feminine activities. Women supplied the needs of their households, and they could even be associated together in shops, under the supervision of a "directress of weavers," to sell their output. Loincloths and dresses were of linen, a supple, light, and lasting material, warm in winter and cool in summer, depending on whether the weave was tight or loose. The cloth most widely used was white or beige, with a simple weft. Linen had the further advantage of being inexpensive because flax was cultivated everywhere in Egypt. Moreover, scenes of pulling up bunches of flax often take place under the expert eye of women who even at this point can appreciate the quality of the material they will have to work with. Wool was known; for goats and sheep were raised. But it was seldom used for making clothes, no doubt because its animal origin made it taboo.

Fashion changed little during the age of the pyramids and does not seem to have been a sign of social class. Men went barechested and wore a short loincloth, a simple, rectangular piece of material wrapped around the waist; it ended above the knees and was held in place by a knot at the waist (Figure 18). Some professional groups had specific costumes. The vizier wore a long, starched skirt that went up to his underarms and was held up by a string around his neck. Temple personnel had to cover their shoulders with a leopard skin while performing cult rituals; perhaps this recalled the animal skins with which people covered themselves in earliest times.

Women wore a long, skin-tight sheath dress held under their breasts by two shoulder straps. This was a traditional costume, worn by goddesses in their representations on temple walls until the end of the pharaonic era. It emphasized the slenderness of the female form but does not seem well suited to daily work. At court, elegant ladies were sometimes dressed in V-necked tunics with long sleeves which displayed a rather elaborate sewing technique. A light shawl also covered their shoulders when the evenings were a little cool. Certain articles of clothing testify to an accomplished art of fashion, despite the rudimentary tools at the disposal of designers. Cloth had to be cut with sharp blades and sewn with bone or bronze needles that were thick and scarcely practical. This was the same set of tools used for putting

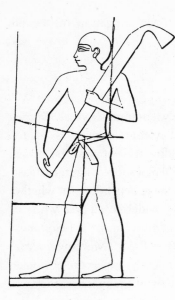

FIGURE 18.
Clothing and hair styles of the Old Kingdom. From mastabas at Abusir and Giza. After C. R. Lepsius, Denkmaeler aus Aegypten und Aethiopien *(Berlin: Nicolai, 1849–56), Part 2, Plates 4 and 21.*

together the parts of the sandals some wore on their feet. Most Egyptians went barefoot, both at home and outdoors. It is not until the second half of the second millennium that we often see a unique form of sandal, composed of a sole of papyrus fibers, palm bark, or leather, to which were attached two leather straps that passed between the toes.

HAIR

Frequently represented in the reliefs and paintings, hair care was an integral part of grooming and the object of daily attention. Hairdressing skills were much in demand, and those who had them could play an important role in the great households in which they were employed. Men and women could choose between keeping their hair natural or wearing a wig, a costume generally reserved for important occasions. Men either wore their hair short and combed back, leaving the ears uncovered, or had a layered cut that covered their head and ears like a round cap made up of short, curled little locks. The latter was perhaps a wig, because the hair of the Egyptians was naturally rather sleek and unsuited to such regular curls. For festivals and ceremonies, they adorned themselves with a mid-length wig parted in the middle, dividing it into two symmetrical sections that hung down to the shoulders. Certain statues show the natural roots underneath this thick hair, indicating that it is indeed a wig.

Women's vanity applied to the care of their natural hair as much as to the wearing of wigs. At the royal court, women had their hair done during breakfast, as depicted in a charming scene on the sarcophagus of princess Kawit (c. 2060 B.C.E.). While a servant hands her a bowl of milk, saying, "To your health, mistress," a young servant girl busies herself with the lady's fine, curly wig, fastening the curls with hairpins; from some examples found in tombs, we know these could be of wood, bone, or ivory. The princess holds a mirror, which enables her to supervise the operations as she eats and to take stock of the results before attending to her duties as mistress of the house. The style of Kawit's wig is rather like a man's: short and curly, it covers her forehead while leaving her ears free, and it sits on her head like a little helmet. The other type of female wig was the traditional hair style of goddesses; its three straight sections framed the face, and it hung all the way down to the breast. Women wore their hair long, and they sometimes braided and rolled it. As for girls, they often had long tresses with a ball-shaped barrette at the end, and they made artful use of their hair in exhibitions of dancing (see Figure 22).

A wigmaker's studio dating approximately to the first half of the second millennium has been discovered at Deir el-Bahri in Upper Egypt. All the items needed for making wigs were assembled and lying on the ground, ready for use: alabaster vases filled with hair, ready-made tresses combining natural hair and plant fibers, as well as a chest made of papyrus for storing pins, needles, and flint knives. The most striking object of this find was a sculpted model of a head serving as a mannequin, on which the wigmaker had marked in black the points where the wigs were to be attached.

Wide-toothed combs of bone or wood were used to comb the hair, and warm beeswax or resin was applied to the tresses to hold the waves of the hairstyle in place. Hair care entailed much use of pomades and lotions intended to make it soft and shiny. Prescriptions for dyeing hair and fighting baldness reveal that such preoccupations were already very much on the minds of the Egyptian population in the third millennium. Moreover, signs of old age are nearly always absent from representations of people; Egyptians preferred to gain immortality bearing the features of youth.

COSMETICS AND UNGUENTS

Once dressed and with their hair taken care of, Egyptians were still not done with their grooming. The smallest festivity was an excuse to take their perfumes, cosmetics, makeup, and jewels out of their wooden or papyrus chests. Unguents had a base of vegetable or animal oil; fragrant with myrrh, terebinth, or incense, they were used to soften the skin and impart a pleasant scent. As early as the predynastic period, oil and unguent containers assumed forms inspired by the world of plants and animals: vases in the form of a female monkey holding her young one to her breast; a vase representing two ducks back to back, with their curved necks forming the handles; a little schist makeup cup imitating a wickerwork basket. Even the most humble baked-clay makeup containers display careful decoration and refined workmanship.

Men and women wore eye makeup, most often outlining their lids with a line of black kohl, a fine powder obtained by crushing galena extracted from the mountains on the Red Sea shore. Kohl enhanced the gaze while protecting the eyes against ophthalmic diseases and infections caused by flies. Egyptians colored their hair, the palms of their hands, the soles of their feet, and their nails with powdered henna, which imparted a deep red color; numerous mummies of women and children bear traces of it, indicating that this usage was traditional. Moreover, it continues in our own times, in the Egyptian countryside.

JEWELRY FOR EVERYDAY WEAR

Serving as both adornment and magical protection, jewels were essentials of daily life for men and women on the banks of the Nile. From the humblest to the most noble, everyone wore them, carved from a great variety of materials. From prehistoric times on, beads, rings, and collars were made from bones, shells, hippopotamus or elephant ivory, crocodile teeth, stone, faience, or simple straps of leather. Gold, which was mined in the eastern deserts and Nubia, also appeared quite early; considered a gift of the gods, and sometimes even one of the many aspects of divine flesh, it was the privilege of the great and adorned the necks and arms of Pharaoh and his court. Pharaonic jewelers had no knowledge of precious stones, such as diamonds and rubies, but they made extensive use of gemstones, producing jewels that were delicate and multicolored, including the orange of carnelian, the mauve of amethyst, the greens of turquoise and feldspar, or again, the deep blue of lapis lazuli. To these we must add jasper, garnet, and rock crystal, all extracted from the deserts of the southeast of the country; on the shores of the Red Sea, shells furnishing an iridescent mother-of-pearl were gathered.

The most common items of jewelry were the collar, the bracelet, and the anklet, whose use was widespread by the beginning of the third millennium. Even when they labored in the fields, Egyptians did not put away their humble ornamental fetishes made of multicolored beads and leather straps. The work of the goldsmiths was destined for the royal family and their courtiers; a treasure trove of the goldsmith's art was discovered in the tomb of the lady Hetepheres, Khufu's mother, who died around 2550 B.C.E. Among her tomb furnishings was found a chest containing about twenty bracelets of silver and ivory decorated with butterflies, ravishing compositions of juxtaposed pieces of turquoise, lapis lazuli, and carnelian.

During the Old Kingdom, the large *usekh*-collar, made of several rows of cylindrical beads of blue or green faience, quickly became the general fashion. A little later, beads were replaced by amulets or by necklaces consisting of a simple thread decorated with one large bead in the middle. Princes and princesses wore "pectorals," large, rectangular plaques that adorned the chest and displayed an openwork, multicolored decoration combining hieroglyphs, plants, and symbols of royalty in various colors and materials.

To hold their wigs in place, women put a hair band around their foreheads; on crowned heads, these took on the appearance of diadems. A simple ribbon into which a water lily was slipped on festive days, the hair band was an essential element of stylish dress, as evidenced by the numerous examples found in the Middle Kingdom tombs of princes and princesses buried at Dahshur and el-Lisht. In these cases, the ribbon is of gold set with inlaid motifs: daisies, little fish or birds, rosettes of turquoise or lapis lazuli, subtly recalling the barrettes hooked along the tresses of a wig.

Worn on bracelets, pendants, and rings, good-luck amulets protected the little Egyptian from birth. Generally, they consisted of a single hieroglyphic sign, made of stone or faience, signifying "life," "health," "endurance," "youth," "stability," or "prosperity," qualities people hoped to secure for themselves by wearing these little magical objects. Egyptians wore simple rings on their fingers, or better, a "scarab" set and mounted on a pivoting setting. In the Middle Kingdom, the flat side of the scarab served as an identification card; on it, carved in stone, we read its owner's name and profession, information always deeply appreciated by the archaeologist. A magical formula for protection or the name of a deity could also be inscribed on the scarab, thus lending the piece of adornment a powerful prophylactic value.

A mirror, the indispensable complement to an impeccable toilette, was an outward sign of wealth. "She who once beheld her face in the water now owns a mirror," we read in a nostalgic text describing the upheavals that beset Egyptian society at the end of the third millennium. Made of copper and later of bronze, mirrors were thin, slightly oblong disks whose surface was polished to the point where the reflection caused no distortion of the face. Their handles were charmingly decorated; carved of wood, ivory, or even of metal, they drew their inspiration from the plant world, assuming the form of a papyrus umbel, or a bundle of leaves, when they did not bear the image of the head of Hathor herself, the goddess of love.

MEALS

Daily chores were not occasions for going to a lot of trouble with one's appearance and taking out all one's finery. Everyday clothing was reduced to the simplest elements of the adornment described above and was not supposed to get in the way of routine activities, of which the most frequent, in every household, was the preparation of meals.

Except in years when the inundation was bad or political disturbance led to administrative disorder, everyone had something to eat in ancient Egypt. There were certainly differences in quality and quantity according to social class, but on the whole, the land was sufficiently fertile and prosperous for everyone to have enough food. The Egyptians seem to have eaten three meals a day; those in the morning and evening were the most substantial, whereas the midday meal could be nothing more than a simple snack for peasants laboring in the fields. Dinner is often mentioned in the texts; it was the most pleasant meal, the one shared by the family in the cool air of dusk. Tomb representations regularly show scenes of meals, but these are funerary meals intended to satisfy all the tastes of the deceased, supplying a large variety of food that surely did not constitute the daily fare of the Egyptians. We can, however, use these scenes to deduce the subtleties of the culinary art in pharaonic Egypt and appreciate its diversity. Some scenes of

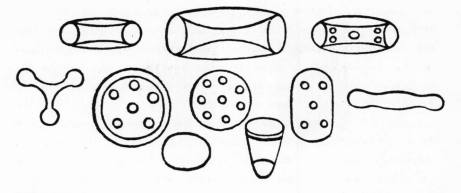

FIGURE 19.

Bread loaves of various shapes. From a Middle Kingdom tomb at Beni Hasan. After C. R. Lepsius, Denkmaeler aus Aegypten und Aethiopien *(Berlin: Nicolai, 1849–56), Part 2, Plates 126, 128, and 129.*

picnics organized on the occasion of hunting and fishing parties give us a better idea of an ordinary meal, frugal and convivial.

Every meal was based on the essentials, bread and beer, both made of the same grains, barley and starchy wheat. Traces suggest the existence of large bakeries, but in general, bread making was the work of the women of the house. Bent over their millstones, they ground the grain until it was a freely pouring flour, which they then sifted. Next, they kneaded the dough, mixing the flour with yeast, milk, salt, and spices. The dough was divided into small, round heaps that rose in the sun on the doorstep. It could also be poured into molds, for a particular shape while baking, a flat or round loaf, for example (Figure 19). A relief of the Old Kingdom displays nineteen kinds of bread, ranging from the rustic flat cake to the white and sugared conical loaf and including oval and square shapes; in each case, the taste must have been slightly different. In this period, bread was baked on the kitchen hearth, which was a slab set on three stones. Later, in the Middle Kingdom, a tall, cylindrical oven made of brick was used. Once baked, the bread was spread with a purée of favas or other beans; with beer, the drink favored by the Egyptians, it constituted the classic meal.

The preparation of beer also fell to the women. Numerous statuettes show these brewers treading on the dough, supervising the fermentation, or filtering the liquid, whose sugar content was raised by adding the juice of dates. Beer, too, came in many varieties; it seems that the dark ones were more common than the light ones, which were reserved for festive meals.

Besides beer, which was unsuitable for children, Egyptians drank milk from cows, goats, ewes, and donkeys. Milk was a part of the daily fare, in liquid form or well curdled and salted. This milk pap, accompanied by bread and onions, figured regularly in the food rations distributed to the workers at construction sites and in the quarries. Wine was also drunk, but only rarely, for viticulture requires a particular soil and care. Wealthier Egyptians imported their wine from the delta, the Faiyum, or the oases of the western desert, in jars duly labeled to indicate their origin, vineyard, and date. Certain great farms of the Nile valley had their own vines, attached to trellises, and supplied a yield sufficient for their household feasts. In the Old Kingdom, there were already six qualities of wine, distinguished by their place of origin, but the most common was a red obtained from a thick, black muscat grape.

From this period on, tomb walls display a great many scenes of fishing and butchery, which we must consult to discover how meat and fish were prepared. For now, it is difficult to appreciate pharaonic gastronomy; for no one has yet discovered a proper papyrus cookbook to bring to light the recipes of the finer tables of the Nile valley.

Meat, less common than fish, was most often prepared in a stew by the women of the house. Meats from domesticated stock included pork, goat, mutton, and beef; desert game included the antelope, the ibex, and the gazelle. When an animal was slaughtered, the meat was carved and cut into pieces that were dried or boiled to make them keep longer. At Abusir, excavations have uncovered the slaughterhouse annex of the funerary temple of the pharaoh Raneferef, who died in 2485 B.C.E. and was buried in his nearby pyramid. In this locale, called the "house of the knife" in the texts, men busied themselves with the sacrifice of animals, mostly bulls, and with the preparation of the meat necessary for the funerary cult of the deceased pharaoh. In the slaughterhouse, large limestone blocks enabled the butchers to keep the animals hobbled and tethered while they cut their throats with a clean, precise stroke of the knife. The ceremony was the same in village butcheries, but meat consumption was lower; indeed a papyrus from the archives of this temple at Abusir informs us that no fewer than 130 bulls were sacrificed in a period of ten days. Such a quantity of meat was not lost to the world; for after performing their cult rituals and making the offerings, the priests were allowed to divide up the food for the benefit of their families. Birds, raised and force-fed in the poultry yards of farms and great estates, contributed a substantial complement of meat: pigeons, cranes, ducks, and geese were very much appreciated and, it seems, affordable to the humble. As for desert game, it ruled the menu of the great tables: its top-quality meat was eaten well roasted on important occasions. Glowing embers were prepared outdoors, and the cooks put the animal on a spit that turned it over the fire. We find the same method of cooking in the preparation of fish; the marshes and canals supplied the fishermen with such good catches that fish were rather commonly consumed. They were seasoned with herbs and spices: anise, dill, fennel, coriander, cumin, and thyme figured as ingredients in the best recipes in addition to their function in making remedies. Fat for cooking came from four kinds of animals, and oil was extracted from sesame, flax, and castor-oil seeds, the best coming from moringa seeds. Honey was a luxury item because hives were rare; when it was lacking, dates could also be used to sweeten food.

Onions, favas, and other beans were the basic vegetables for everyday meals, but other varieties were sometimes picked in the kitchen gardens: garlic, green peas, lettuce, leeks, lentils, and cucumbers were the object of meticulous care by the gardeners on agricultural estates. Orchards supplied fruits in quantity; also cultivated, in addition to the vine, were figs and dates, whose nutritional value was recognized very early.

Before every meal, the family washed their hands, pouring water from a ewer set near the dishes: rich and poor alike ate with their fingers, and the ewer, which was also used at the end of the meal, was invariably present. It seems that at the beginning of the third millennium, people ate sitting directly on the floor. The family sat on a rush mat, with a large platter in the center on which the foods were arranged; with the fingers, each person took his or her fill. Progressively, as Egyptian civilization developed, the custom of taking meals while seated at a table became more widespread. Beginning with the Fifth Dynasty (c. 2500 B.C.E.), low tables appeared, as well as higher pedestal tables at which guests sat in pairs, while children remained squatting on the ground. Though families ate together a great deal, with all ages and both sexes mingled, we never observe scenes of families seated around a single table, the four-legged table being unknown in ancient Egypt. Even today, Egyptians in the countryside eat on the ground, work sitting cross-legged, and stay squatting at the door of their homes or under a tree to chat with their friends.

Ordinary dishes were of baked clay; it was the village potter who turned them on his wheel, using clay collected on the banks of the river, and baked them in the town hearth. Archaeological sites abound in sherds of undecorated, coarse ware, which was made of a thick, brownish paste and the purpose of which was to hold the food of the Egyptians of antiquity. Stoneware, which was the work of skilled, sophisticated artisans, seems not to have been much used in daily life. Rather, it was employed in the furnishings of tombs: dishes of stone and fine, decorated baked clay were reserved for offerings intended for the dead. It is thanks to this custom that we can admire in museums today the most accomplished side of the pharaonic ceramic craft, which in fact rather distorts our idea of everyday wares.

LEISURE AND RECREATION

Even if families largely used their time working in the fields or in the home, there was still a little to devote to leisure. Egyptian civilization early displayed its taste for games and recreation: the oldest examples of board games found in excavations date to the First Dynasty.

The simplest form of recreation was an excursion, whether on foot, in a litter with bearers, or in a boat. When attending to some business on his domain, an owner of estates could make use of an outing to the countryside to take the family along, accompanied by servants and assistants. The boat or the litter was reserved for the most important family members; the rest of the band made their way on foot. Thus when princess Idut (c. 2400 B.C.E.) made a pleasure tour of the canals in the marshes, she remained in her boat accompanied by her nurse and a servant, while nineteen persons escorted her on the bank. The court notables Ty and Ptahhotpe preferred a litter, which they occupied alone (Figure 20). Four or more men were needed to carry, on their shoulders, the shafts which bore the chair with its back. The owner took his seat with an air of importance and ordered his available servants to hold out parasols on either side of the chair to protect him from the sun. To raise their spirits and lend a regular rhythm to the progress of the retinue, the men sang in chorus. The words of these songs are often carved above the scenes representing the master on his excursion; eager to flatter their boss, the bearers chant, "Joyous are those who carry the chair! It is more pleasant when it is filled than when it is empty! Forward, comrades, to protect the one who is in good health!"

Dogs ran freely hither and thither, playing with monkeys on leashes; they would take part in the incidents of hunting or fishing that an outing might occasion. At home or on an excursion, pets were the best of companions in moments of relaxation. The names given to dogs bear witness to the affection people bore them: "Good Shepherd," "Trusty," "Brave," "Speedy," "Master." From the First Dynasty (c. 3050 B.C.E.) on, Egyptians carefully buried their dogs; stone stelae carved with the names of dogs have been

FIGURE 20.

Ty being carried in a litter; the upper portion of the scene is now lost. From his Old Kingdom mastaba at Saqqara. After Lucienne Épron, François Daumas, Georges Goyon, and Pierre Montet, Le Tombeau de Ti, Mémoires publiés par les membres de l'Institut Français d'Archéologie Orientale du Caire 65, fascicle 1 *(Cairo: Institut Français d'Archéologie Orientale du Caire: 1939), Plate XVI. © IFAO. Reproduced by permission of the Institut Français d'Archéologie Orientale du Caire.*

found in the archaic cemeteries of Abydos in Upper Egypt. One pharaoh went so far as to issue a decree at the death of his dog: "His majesty commands that the dog be buried and that he be given a coffin from the Double House of the Treasury, and cloth, incense, and sacred oil."

BOARD GAMES

Evenings at home were spent quietly, on the rooftop terrace or on the doorstep. People breathed the cool night air and amused themselves with some game of solitaire, chance, or strategy. In addition to their everyday recreational aspect, board games were endowed with a religious-funerary connotation: people had themselves buried with checkerboards, jacks, and gaming pieces to gamble for their destiny beyond the tomb with the invisible forces of the hereafter. Consequently, it was useful to practice while still alive. One of the most popular games was *senet*, the ancestor of the trictrac of the modern East. The two players sat on either side of a board with thirty squares and moved their pieces, which were cones decorated with animals or people. The boards could be traced on the ground or the paving or made of stone, baked clay, or wood — in the last case, forming the upper part of a box with a drawer in which the pieces were stored. At archaeological sites, it is not rare to recognize a limestone splinter on which a little, unknown hand has scratched a game board, and it is then difficult to tell whether this object is ancient or of the twentieth century of our own era!

Another game with dice and gaming pieces was *mehen*, or the serpent game. It was played on a small, circular table that assumed the form of a coiled serpent wound around its own head and engraved with squares alternately sunken and in relief. Six people could play, each player having three pieces in the form of lions, three in the form of lionesses, and six marbles of different colors. On a wall of the tomb of Kayemankh (c. 2340 B.C.E.) at Saqqara, we see young people devoting themselves to the serpent game. One of them impatiently says, "Hurry up!" to his embarrassed partner, who has spent too much time thinking. The rules of the game are lost, but they seem to have been similar to those of our snakes and ladders or, better still, to those of a game still played in the Sudan, the "game of the hyena." In the Middle Kingdom, beginning around 2060, the game of hounds and jackals was a favorite of the Egyptians. It was played by two people, each one having a series of six pegs made of bone and ending in dogs' or jackals' heads, which the player moved on a tray pierced by evenly spaced holes. The tray itself could have an animal form: the one in the Louvre is a flattened hippopotamus; the pegs were placed in its back.

MUSIC, SONG, AND DANCE

In the temples, rituals were traditionally accompanied by music and dance; but these arts were not restricted to such use. In private life, they also provided entertainment at important family events and at the secular gatherings and banquets that enlivened the life of the villages. The "Maxims of Ptahhotpe," a compendium of sage advice on how to live like a good Egyptian, places considerable emphasis on worldly pleasures: "Do not shorten the time devoted to pleasure, . . . do not lose time in daily work when you have done what is necessary for your house. When your fortune is made, follow your desire; for a fortune has no interest if one is glum." We should not allow the apparent ubiquity of the divine in the Egyptian world to hide the fact that individuals nurtured a real anxiety about the afterlife and had the courage to live happy moments on earth to the full. That, moreover, is the sense of the "Harper's Song," the very popular tune that musicians would strike up at banquets to encourage the guests to think of death only to forget it and enjoy the present moment. This scene, represented many times on the walls of private tombs, includes the best-known verses of this

FIGURE 21.

Old Kingdom harp and flutes. From mastabas at Saqqara and Giza. After C. R. Lepsius, Denkmaeler aus Aegypten und Aethiopien *(Berlin: Nicolai, 1849–56), Part 2, Plates 61a and 74.*

poem set to music: "No one has come back from below to tell us their condition, to tell us their needs, to comfort our hearts. . . . Rejoice while you are alive, . . . follow your heart and your happiness . . . for lamentations save no one from the pit!"

This refrain, accompanied by their instrument alone, was undoubtedly the most classic song in the harpers' repertoire. The harp was associated with carnal pleasures, for its sweet melody aroused couples to love. Thus Mereruka, son-in-law of the pharaoh Teti (c. 2340 B.C.E.), asked his wife, the charming princess Watet-Khethor, to play him a tune on the harp while he prepared for bed.

Large, organized orchestras would appear in the New Kingdom (1552–1070 B.C.E.), but in the period treated here, music was confined essentially to a song, solo or in chorus, supported by one or two instruments (Figure 21). A conductor led the playing, indicating by the position of his hands the pitch to give, the note to play, and the rhythm to follow. We would love to know the sounds that came from these groups, but unfortunately the Egyptians had no system of musical notation, thus making any reconstruction of their music purely hypothetical and imaginary. Besides the harp and the lyre, the latter imported from Asia, wind instruments made from reeds, wood, or metal are commonly represented. Flutes and reed instruments are the most widespread; we see them with one or two pipes, and with holes varying in number from three to five. Percussion instruments, indispensable accompaniments in scenes of dancing, belonged in every household: the female dancers would click their clappers together while stamping their feet and twirling around, as is still the fashion in Andalusia, with castanets. In the countryside, harvesters and grape pickers set out for the fields with several pairs of clappers, with which they would accompany themselves as they sang to raise their spirits and to help them sustain the pace of work and maintain a good rhythm. We encounter this same custom today at excavation sites, when one of the workers, the bard of the group, sets his basket on the ground and, clapping his hands, chants a lively tune, which the others take up in chorus, not knowing that their forebears once worked up a semblance of enthusiasm in the same way. Many clappers have been found among tomb furnishings; they are of wood, bone, or ivory and take the form of hands or forearms, recalling that they are an instrumental transposition of the gesture of clapping the hands. Their widely attested presence in tombs is undoubtedly due to the magical value attributed to them in Egyptian belief; by striking the clappers, evil spirits were put to flight, and the deceased was protected in eternal rest.

Without doubt, we must give this same magical interpretation to the discovery of the earliest drum from ancient Egypt, which was found in a tomb dating to the Middle Kingdom (c. 2000 B.C.E.). This drum, a simple cylindrical barrel of palm wood covered with stretched skin at both ends, was placed near the coffin as a thunderous accessory for the passage to the hereafter. In the second millennium, drums and tabors would play a part in all festivities, religious or secular.

At banquets and other private entertainments, exhibitions of dance were performed by very young girls, who moved in harmony, after the fashion of a ballet. They swayed gracefully, their hair flying in the wind, making jerking and darting movements, sometimes on their toes (Figure 22). The "mirror dance" represented a complex choreography in the course of which the girls held a mirror whose handle evoked the figure of Hathor, goddess of love, joy, and drunkenness. In these scenes, one girl distinguishes herself from the group by more acrobatic movement: she is the principal dancer of the ballet troupe.

Guests at banquets were also fond of another spectacle, fights among men. Both game and sport, the fight was the opportunity for young men to highlight their dexterity and train for combat. Ptahhotpe (c. 2400 B.C.E.) had one of these scenes represented on a wall of his mastaba: the fighters faced one another in pairs, grasped one another's body with their arms, and were to make their opponent lose his balance, until one of them was the first to fall defeated. Then the winner confronted the champion of the next pair, until the final match between the two best. To the great satisfaction of the spectators, the holds were rather brutal; one of them, it so happened, even had to be carried out, wounded, on a stretcher. The most famous fight scene is painted on a wall of the tomb of Khety (c. 2000 B.C.E.), a regional

FIGURE 22.

Female dancers. From the Middle Kingdom tomb of Khety at Beni Hasan. After Jean-François Champollion, Monuments de l'Égypte et de la Nubie, *Volume IV (Paris: Imprimerie et Librarie de Firmin Didot Frères, 1845), Plate CCCLXVII.*

administrator of the province of Beni Hasan (Figure 23). There, in five superimposed registers, we can admire 219 pairs of fighters heatedly grappling with one another. In this period, such fighting was not regarded solely as an entertainment but, rather, as physical training for the military life that the young men under Khety's administration would have to experience.

At Pharaoh's court, the most refined amusements were the entertainments performed by pygmies brought at great cost from the heart of Africa. Their unusual bodies astonished and amused, while the African freedom and rhythm of their swaying movements lent their dance an exotic character much in demand by the sovereign's associates. A letter written by young Pepy II (c. 2200 B.C.E.) attests to the attraction of these precious little dancers. Quite excited over the imminent arrival at court of a new Pygmy, whom a high official named Harkhuf had sought out in the region of Dongola, the king asks his official to take very good care of him: "Come, then, by boat to the Residence immediately. Leave the others and bring this dwarf . . . you

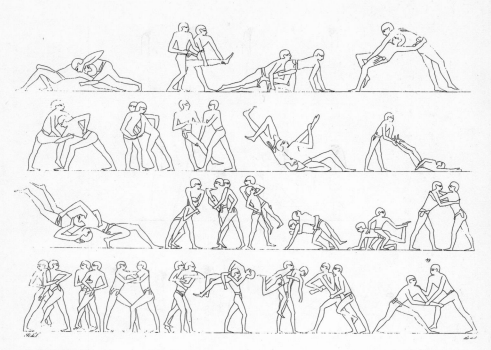

FIGURE 23.

Some of the 219 pairs of fighters depicted in the Middle Kingdom tomb of Khety at Beni Hasan. After Hippolito Rosellini, Monumenti dell'Egitto e della Nubia, Volume II (Pisa: Presso Niccolò Capurro e C., 1832), Plate CXII.

are bringing back . . . for the dances of the gods . . . and to delight the heart of the king. . . . If he boards the boat with you, station able men . . . on both sides of the boat to prevent him from falling into the water. If he sleeps at night, station able men to sleep around him in his cabin. Have rounds made ten times a night." The Pygmy would arrive safe and sound, and the festival could begin at the royal palace.

8　LIFE IN THE COUNTRY

Egypt was born of the Nile, but surely it could only have survived and prospered by the extraordinary zeal with which Egyptians exploited to the fullest the agricultural boon their river brought them. The country derived the greater part of its riches from the close symbiosis of sun, water, and people, which permitted a varied food production equal to the needs of its population. Early on, mastery of the water and control of irrigation — natural, and later artificial — became the preoccupation of all, from the peasant in his field to the high official in his government office. Winning ground from the vast, inhospitable desert and maintaining ever more surface area of "black land," rich and heavy with silt, in the valley were the avowed goals. The cultivated surface area has been estimated at nearly 3,100 square miles at the time of the pyramids. Only in the twentieth century of our own era, with the considerable advances from construction of the High Dam at Aswan, has the figure increased massively, in recent years to well over 15,000 square miles.

THE NILE INUNDATION

In the eyes of the Egyptians, the inundation appeared as a tangible sign of divine activity, which alone was capable of this life-giving miracle. But when the flood was too low, it bore witness to the anger of the supreme powers, who had decided to produce a famine. A bad inundation was always the greatest curse the peasant had to fear, whereas the exuberant manifestations of joy at the arrival of the first muddy, silt-filled water around July 20 proclaim the relief this rise in the waters accorded to the hearts of the Egyptians. A "Hymn to the Nile," several versions of which are provided in manuscripts of the New Kingdom, though the date of its composition is unknown, expresses this anticipation: "Hail to you, oh Nile, sprung from the ground, come to keep the land alive, . . . who inundates the fields that Re has created to make all the animals live, . . . who produces barley and makes wheat grow, that the temples might be in festival. If he is sluggish, noses suffocate, everyone is impoverished. . . . If he rises, the land is in exultation, and everyone is in joy." The fourteen strophes of this text glorify this spirit Nile-Hapy, personification of the inundation, whose wrath was feared and who was showered with praise and gifts. Until the beginning of the present century, the Egyptians retained some memory of the ancient rituals and practices, and each time the waters rose anew, they would perpetuate millennia-old pagan traditions. The inundation was the occasion of a national festival that brought all Egyptians to the banks of their river, into which they cast offerings of flowers, food, and — more symbolically — dolls intended to arouse his desire to swell up and inundate the land.

YEARS OF "LEAN CATTLE"

Famines were the direct consequence of what the texts call a "low Nile." When they occurred, these bad years long remained engraved in the collective memory. The rich took advantage of them to emphasize their continued feeding of their communities despite the alarming condition of the supplies in their granaries. Ameny, chief of the Oryx province in Middle Egypt, had the following text carved on a wall of his tomb at Beni Hasan at the beginning of the second millennium: "I was compassionate, benevolent, and always beloved, a governor loved by his subjects. . . . I did not scorn any daughter of the people, I did not oppress any widow, I did not rebuff any peasant, I did not turn away any herdsman. . . . There was no poor man in my surroundings; no one died of hunger in my time. When the years of famine came, I had all the fields of my province plowed as far as its northern and southern borders, and I sustained its inhabitants; I gave them something to eat, and no one went hungry in my province. I gave as much to the widow as to the wife, and I made no distinction between the humble and the great in my allocations. Then abundant Niles came, bringing barley and wheat, rich in all good things; but I exacted nothing as outstanding taxes on the harvest." When they could not count on so generous a governor, the poor asked all their relatives scattered throughout the country to send them food. Heqanakhte, a priest sent on a mission to the north of the land around 2000 B.C.E., wrote thus to his family remaining in Thebes: "I arrived here and collected as much food for you as possible. The Nile, is it not in fact very low? And the food we have collected is proportionate to the flood. . . . Here, one has begun to eat people. Nowhere is there someone to whom nourishment is given. You must hold out until my return: I intend to spend the season of *shemu* (March to July) here."

THE INUNDATION SEASON

It was the Nile that set the rhythm of agricultural life, fixing the schedule of the peasant's tasks according to its ebb and flow. The three seasons of the year each bore the name of the agricultural phenomenon dominating the period in question. The first season (*akhet*), from mid-July to mid-November, was the Inundation. The peasant could stay home then, in that time of the year when the sun blazed and he appreciated the shade of his house. The river did the work for him, slowly invading the countryside and soaking the cracked earth with rich, moist soil. It was then that he took advantage of the free time to repair his tools or make new ones for the plowing to come.

Paintings and bas-reliefs in the tombs show that the peasant's equipment was rudimentary. His hoe was made of a blade of hard wood inserted into a handle and tied to it with a cross piece of braided rope. Derived from the hoe but larger in size, the plow could produce a straight furrow in the wet ground. This rudimentary form of plow was drawn by a man or a team of oxen, while the plowman opened the soil by pushing and guiding the share deep into it. A wooden sickle was used to reap the grain; it was gently curved, its upper part split along its length and set with flint teeth both sharp and easy to replace. Even after the appearance of bronze at the beginning of the Middle Kingdom, the Neolithic tool kit was long retained, and objects of flint, a hard and sharp stone, are often found in later archaeological material. Thus at Balat in el-Dakhla Oasis, the excavations at the townsite from the end of the Old Kingdom yielded an important batch of flint tools — blades, picks, hammers, and polishers — all side by side with tools of metal, which were more in demand and more expensive. Hard stone was also employed to cut wood, which was used to make all the equipment for winnowing and gathering: sieves, pitchforks, rakes, and bushels. The bags and nets serving as containers for grain were made of plant fibers, leather, or cloth; the women lent a hand in making them.

During the inundation season, the peasants went about in boats of papyrus, and from their crafts they surveyed the height of the waters and the strength of the dikes and reservoirs. At the season's end, they were able to gather a little strength before returning to their work, which, if we are to believe the descriptions handed down in literary texts, was exhausting. To encourage his son to enter the public school and induce him to learn the noble profession of scribe, Khety (c. 2000 B.C.E.) described the hard life of the peasant to him in his celebrated "Satire of the Trades": "The peasant groans unceasingly; his sound is harsh, like the cawing of a raven. His fingers and his arms suppurate and stink to excess. He is weary from standing in the mud, clothed in rags and tatters. . . . When he leaves his field and returns home in the evening, he arrives thoroughly exhausted from the walk."

This literary genre, designed to exalt the scribal profession while disparaging the labors of illiterate peasants, originated in the Middle Kingdom, along with the emergence of an important middle class in the offices of the pharaonic administration; it was deemed necessary to instill disgust at the possibility of returning to the land. Besides the filth and fatigue intrinsic to the peasant's work, these compositions recall the difficulties and nuisances with which nature threatened every cultivator: a bad inundation, a hailstorm, a swarm of locusts, pilfering birds, an invasion of mice and rats, and unexpected visits by livestock enclosed in neighboring pastures, not to mention the forays of starved hippopotamuses greedily helping themselves in the fields as soon as the peasant had his back turned.

The peasant was not the owner of his plot of land; in principle, Pharaoh himself was sole lord of the fields, the temples, and the towns. To exploit the land, he entrusted its administration and management to landholders drawn from the nobility and the upper middle class, and these recruited an abundant personnel who were employed on their estates. At harvest time, the state dispatched scribal civil servants to the locales to deduct that part which went into the public treasury (Figure 24), leaving the rest to the landholder, who in his turn would distribute their rations to the peasants as wages for their work. "A little sheaf per day, that is all I receive for my work," complained a peasant as he mowed the wheat. There is no doubt that everyone had something to eat in ancient Egypt, but one's daily bread was more or less abundant depending on status.

ARTIFICIAL IRRIGATION

Historians continue to debate the date of the first steps toward artificial irrigation, which created a network of secondary canals intended to con-

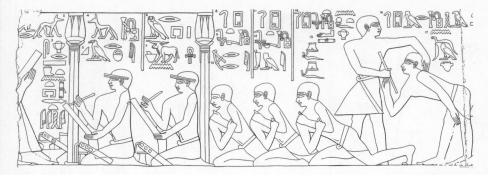

FIGURE 24.
Village headmen being brought to the scribes to pay the harvest tax. After The
Sakkarah Expedition, The Mastaba of Mereruka, *The University of Chicago*
Oriental Institute Publications 31 (Chicago: The University of Chicago Press,
1938), Part I, Plate 37. Courtesy of The Oriental Institute of The University of
Chicago.

duct water into areas won from the desert, which the inundation would not
naturally reach. Nevertheless, the digging of canals is represented on very
ancient documents. The mace-head of King Scorpion, one of the pharaohs
of the earliest dynasty at the end of the fourth millennium, portrays this
sovereign, hoe in hand, ready to open a breach in a retaining wall, while a
man presents him with a basket that perhaps contained plants or sheaves of
wheat. But the interpretation of this fragmentary document is highly uncer-
tain, and today there is agreement in thinking that the canals attested in the
Old Kingdom owed their existence solely to the convenience they afforded
in the transportation of heavy loads or the travel of persons in a hurry to
reach their destinations. Until the end of the Old Kingdom, the Egyptians
would remain content to derive good yields from their fields by exploiting
the lands flooded by the inundation and taking advantage of the occasional
rainfalls still somewhat numerous in that period. A series of bad inunda-
tions and an appreciable increase in population at the end of the third millennium caused a change in agricultural techniques and led Pharaoh's government to plan the construction, on a national scale, of retaining basins,
levees, dikes, and irrigation canals.

Thus another Khety, prince of the province of Asyut around 2100 B.C.E.,
boasted of having dug a canal ten cubits (just over seventeen feet) wide, to
supply new lands with water from a reservoir. In the Twelfth Dynasty, at
the beginning of the second millennium, the development of artificial irrigation was a constant concern of both the state and the local communities.

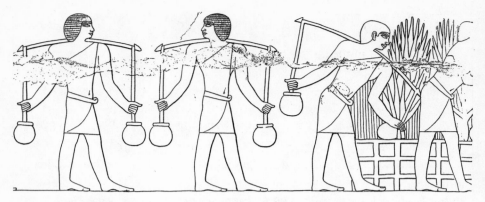

FIGURE 25.

Gardeners watering lettuce. After The Sakkarah Expedition, The Mastaba of Mereruka, *The University of Chicago Oriental Institute Publications 31 (Chicago: The University of Chicago Press, 1938), Part I, Plate 21. Courtesy of The Oriental Institute of The University of Chicago.*

The development of the oasis of the Faiyum and its surrounding country-side by diverting the waters of the Bahr Yusuf, a canal leading from the Nile to the lake of the Faiyum, was one of the great economic successes of the pharaohs of this dynasty. In exploiting the water of Lake Moeris and digging canals that issued from the Bahr Yusuf, the Senwosrets and Amenemhets created a new agricultural province with a prosperous and inviting landscape.

To water his higher fields situated beyond the zone checkered by canals, the peasant of the third millennium made use of a simple board balanced on his shoulders, from either end of which hung a clay jug filled with water drawn from the nearest canal. This rudimentary and toilsome procedure is often shown in the reliefs from Old Kingdom mastabas. Thus in the tomb of Mereruka (c. 2340 B.C.E.), one of the carved scenes depicts gardeners, with planks yoked to their shoulders, bending over their square lettuce patches, carefully watering them; the squares are bounded by relatively high earthen levees that retain the water (Figure 25). Elsewhere, in the tombs of Neankhkhnum and Khnumhotpe (c. 2500 B.C.E.), the watering of vegetables seems to have been specifically an activity of certain convict laborers, who worked at it from dawn to dusk. It was only in the fourteenth century that the *shaduf,* a mechanical device for lifting water which is still seen in the Egyptian countryside, was imported from Mesopotamia.

PLOWING AND SOWING

In November, in the last month of the season *akhet*, the peasants monitored the fall in the water level. Mid-November was the beginning of the season *peret*, Emergence, which saw the river steadily recede into its bed, allowing the fields, which had been saturated and fertilized by the silt, to reappear — or to "emerge," if we translate the Egyptian word literally. This was a time of intense activity in the fields: for not a moment was to be lost in the preparation and maximum exploitation of this soft, wet, heavy soil that was so easy to work. "One desires the inundation, one finds advantage in it; but there is no plowed field that creates itself on its own," a wisdom text of the Twelfth Dynasty correctly recalls. Plowers and sowers traversed the fields and did not hesitate to recruit their wives and children for the busiest days. If the permanent personnel attached to a domain were insufficient, the landowner responsible for the development of the fields could easily hire seasonal laborers — those very men to be found during the inundation on the construction sites of the great works of the state.

The major part of the agricultural lands was devoted to the cultivation of flax and grains, the pursuit most often described on the walls of mastabas in images and words. Much to our amusement, the scenes are annotated by the peasants' conversations, which can turn to wit or insult: men walk in pairs on the wet earth, their feet sinking down to their ankles, busying themselves with the yokes of oxen or cows that draw the plow. One man urges the animals to move forward and plies his whip when shouts no longer suffice, while the other makes the furrow, turning over the soil. "Go on, guide it, hurry, hurry with the oxen! Watch out, the master is there and he's looking," we read in one dialogue. Elsewhere, a peasant boasts, "I'll do even more than the master wishes," while his companion is less zealous: "Hurry and finish your work so we can get home early." The most common invectives directed at the draft animals have surprisingly close resemblances to those of French peasants as they urge their beasts along. "Heave-ho!" was the usual cry the peasant directed at his cows, which he called "workers": "Pull hard, workers! About-face!" The sower, who could be a woman, walked behind or beside the plowmen. He or she carried a sack slung over the shoulder, or a wicker basket in the hand, taking out fistful of seeds that fell like rain into the furrow. Sometimes the earth was so soft there was no point in turning it over, and sowing could proceed without plowing. But sometimes, on the contrary, in areas that had not been long under water, the ground was assailed with a pickax to break up clods that were still hard.

After the sowing, the seeds had to be pressed into the ground, to avoid the raids of birds and to promote a good growth. In this, herdsmen collaborated with the farmers; they came with their flocks of sheep and goats and turned them loose in the field to trample the sowed earth with their quick hooves. The herdsmen, reputed to be good singers, would strike up a nostalgic refrain, of which we have a number of examples: "The herdsman is in the water, in the midst of the fish. He talks with the catfish, he chats with the Nile fish. Oh, West, where is your shepherd?" This couplet expresses the loneliness of the herdsmen, their only companions the fauna of the canals and marshes, as well as their anxiety about the fate awaiting them in the west, on the riverbank of the dead.

By the time the sowing was done, it was the middle of winter. The temperature and the sunshine were ideal for a slow germination of the seeds and a good growth of the ears. Watching over the fields was a daily concern: children were sent to scare off birds swarming down on the growing crops, earthen levees collapsed by the inundation were repaired, and water channels were cleaned out or redeveloped in accordance with the new requirements of the year.

REAPING AND HARVESTING

The heat returned in March. In the middle of the month began the season *shemu,* "Heat," or Dryness, which the inundation would bring to an end in mid-July. This was time for the harvest, which began with the pulling of the flax, gathered while still in bloom to obtain a soft, supple linen. Flax was a raw material highly valued by the Egyptians: clothes for the living were made of it, and shrouds for the dead, as well as cordage, and nets for hunting and fishing; the oil extracted from its seeds was used to make medicinal products. The stalks were pulled with a quick, sure flick of the wrist under the supervision of scribes of the estate, who registered the yield and reckoned up the harvest. The work progressed rapidly, accompanied by the music of a flutist, who lent encouragement to the laborers with his instrument or his voice. His refrain was taken up in chorus by the workers: "Beautiful is the dawn of day that appears over the land; a fresh breeze stirs from the north; the sky complies with our wishes; let us work with a stout heart!" Seated in the shade not far from them, a group of older men and some women tended to the ginning.

After the flax, the grain was reaped: barley and spelt for beer and starchy wheat for bread, the two staples of Egyptian nourishment. At the sight of a bunch of fresh barley, a foreman says, "I tell you, comrades, the barley is ripe, and he who reaps it well will have it." In reaping, the men seized a handful of ears and cut them with a stroke of a sickle, leaving behind a goodly height of stubble, which the livestock would come and graze after the harvest. Here as well, the work was done with a song: one of the reapers, famous for his beautiful voice, puts his sickle under his arm and begins to sing, clapping his hands, while a flutist gives him the pitch. Progressing through the field, the men let the cut sheaves fall to the ground, leaving to the gleaners the task of heaping them up. The job was tedious, and the men worked up a thirst: "Some beer for the one cutting the barley!" one of them cries out. A round of beer, which was stored in a pointed jug, was then passed through the ranks of the reapers. Sometimes the men broke for a snack, eating provisions they had left in the shade in baskets. Reapers in the same field were inspired by a certain rivalry. The first one to finish, standing at the end of his furrow, did not fail to stress his merits: "A guy who works fast, that's me! Who works while talking? Me! Whose chest is tanned and his hands calloused? Me! You, you're lazy!"

Once cut, the sheaves were collected by the gleaners, mostly women and children, who tied them into bundles and heaped them at the end of the field, in large carrying nets. Then the donkeys arrived, trotting quickly as their masters ran behind them, stick in hand, guiding them along. In no time at all, the place was full of dust, shouts, and commotion. The stubborn donkeys would stand rigid at the sight of their burden and refuse to move along. Blows of the stick rained down; it took several people to hold the animal still and load it with double sacks filled to the brim. Finally, the procession could depart for the threshing floor, located not far from the village. Today, threshing floors can still be seen in operation in the Egyptian countryside: they are more or less circular surfaces of ground onto which the sheaves are dumped to be trampled by donkeys or oxen walking endlessly in a circle as the peasants urge them on. "I'll beat you if you stray!" we often read in the annotations to scenes of threshing, which regularly depict donkeys backing up or preferring to eat the fresh sheaves rather than tread them (Figure 26).

The grain then had to be separated from the husk and the impurities. Winnowing was the business of women, who can be recognized by the shawl worn on the head for protection from the dust. They devoted themselves to this task on days when the wind was strong, relying on this natural

FIGURE 26.

Donkeys on a threshing floor. From an Old Kingdom mastaba at Giza. After C. R. Lepsius, Denkmaeler aus Aegypten und Aethiopien *(Berlin: Nicolai, 1849–56), Pl. 9.*

winnowing to carry off the husks as they tossed the grain into the air. A final, general sifting completed the cleaning and enabled the peasants to make a solemn presentation of a measure of the new grain to the master of the domain, who assessed its quality.

Finally, the grain could be stored. The bushels were taken to the granaries, under the strict supervision of scribes of the granary administration, who registered the harvest and calculated the tax the domain would have to pay to the state. Many depictions of granaries dating to the Middle Kingdom disclose what these buildings looked like: granaries were conical in shape and built of unbaked brick covered with plaster. They were approximately sixteen and one-half feet high, with a diameter of about six and one-half feet, and they were lined up in one or two rows in an enclosed court. An upper opening reached by a ladder allowed the storage of the harvest (Figure 27), and a window below was used to draw off the grain as needed. The scribe accountable for the grain stationed himself on a terrace near the upper opening of the granary, so as to be sure not to miss any sack on its way to be poured in.

From the middle of the third millennium on, there was an effort to exploit the land between the end of the grain harvest in April and the return of the inundation in July. This was time enough to plan for other crops, especially vegetables and legumes, which afforded the advantage of enriching the soil with nitrogen. Favas and other beans, lentils, chick-peas, garlic, onions, and leeks were planted, watered, and harvested within these three months.

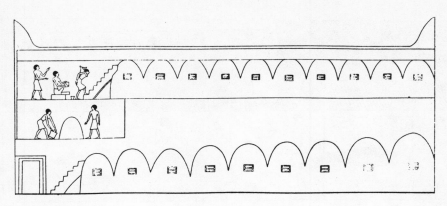

FIGURE 27.

Grain being taken to the granaries. From the Middle Kingdom tomb of Khety at Beni Hasan. After Jean-François Champollion, Monuments de l'Égypte et de la Nubie, *Volume IV (Paris: Imprimerie et Librairie de Firmin Didot Frères, 1845), Plate CCCLXXXI.*

GARDENS, ORCHARDS, AND VINEYARDS

Around the farms and houses, gardens and orchards made the setting more pleasant with their shade and their freshness. Although they required less hard work, they furnished a variety of produce and fruits that, in conjunction with the vines, improved the ordinary fare. Metjen, a high official of the territorial administration of several delta provinces at the beginning of the Fourth Dynasty (c. 2600 B.C.E.), seems to have acquired the usufruct of a beautiful domain, which he describes thus: "a domain 200 cubits (over 340 feet) long and 200 cubits wide, enclosed with walls, well-stocked, planted with beautiful trees . . . with a very large basin . . . planted with fig trees and vines. . . . Wine was produced there in great quantity." These gardens were meticulously tended. The gardener would come regularly and hand water each kind of vegetable, which occupied one or more squares bounded by earthen levees. Thanks to his care, the kitchen gardens were filled all year long with cucumbers, melons, green peas, cabbage, horse-radish, coriander, cumin, parsley, and lastly, lettuce, to which aphrodisiac properties were attributed.

Lovers of flowers, the Egyptians would plant them in their gardens and along the borders of their kitchen gardens, and they presented beautiful bouquets to both the living and the dead. There was almost always a bouquet on the tables of offerings dedicated to the deceased; for Egyptians could not conceive of an existence, in this life or the next, without the sweet

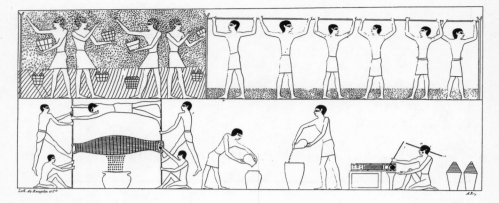

FIGURE 28.

*Grape picking and wine making. From the Middle Kingdom tomb of Khety at
Beni Hasan. After Jean-François Champollion,* Monuments de l'Égypte et de la
Nubie, *Volume IV (Paris: Imprimerie et Librairie de Firmin Didot Frères, 1845),
Plate CCCLXXX.*

perfume and singular color of cornflowers, poppies, chrysanthemums, irises,
hyacinths, mandragoras, larkspurs, water lilies, or jasmine.

Orchards provided a habitat for trees, so rare and valuable in this sun-
scorched land. The Egyptians loved their trees, which they associated with
certain deities. Thus Hathor, goddess of love and music, was called "Mistress of the Sycamore," undoubtedly recalling the benefits this tree provided. Trees were planted along the paths of gardens or grouped in orchards
surrounded by earthen walls. Along with the sycamore grew date palms,
dom palms, and pomegranate and fig trees. The palm trees yielded beautiful
clusters of dates which the children, accompanied by monkeys, would collect each winter, climbing to the tops of the trees to cut the well-ripened
bunches. Some wild species of trees grew here and there on the border between the cultivation and the deserts: this was the locale preferred by acacias, mimosas, tamarisks, and Egyptian willows.

Besides the great vineyards of the land in the delta and in the western
desert oases of el-Dakhla and el-Kharga, which furnished the country's best
vintages, each garden had its vine. The fruit, a very sweet blue-black muscat
grape, was as much appreciated as the wine, which was the drink of festivals and feasts. Some scenes from tombs depict the arbors; there we see that
the long stems are trained over forked stakes, between which the pickers
walked as they collected the ripe grapes (Figure 28). Here too, the schedule
imposed by the river was a great help to the peasants; for in fact the grapes

had to be picked in August and September, when the inundation reached its highest level, making any work in the fields impossible. Picking the grapes was a delicate task; for bunches had to be put one by one into a wicker basket, which was then taken to the winepress. There, the harvested grapes were poured into a large stone vat, above which was a horizontal beam. When the vat was full, the wine makers climbed in and began to trample the grapes in a lively manner. A musician — a flutist or a castanet player — marked the cadence of their work, which was considered grueling because of the odor emanating from the must. When the grapes had yielded all their juice from the treading, the contents of the vat were left to steep for several days, while the sugar of the grapes turned quickly into alcohol. The liquid was then captured in jars placed beneath holes pierced in the bottom of the vat. The skins and the seeds of the grapes were collected in large sacks that were twisted several times by turning sticks slipped into both ends. This wringing process extracted yet a little more of the precious liquid. The wine was then filtered through a fine cloth and left to age in jars stopped with a clay plug. The annotation to one scene illustrating the pouring of the wine into jars is eloquent: "It's completely full! What you've done is good!" The fermentation could take years; the process was always monitored by the wine makers, who paid very special attention to it.

LIVESTOCK FARMING

The breeding and raising of a diversity of animals played an important role in the Egyptian economy from a very early date. Evidently, the domestication of animals was recognized as an excellent means of supplying meat, milk, and hides, but the use of livestock as draft animals in agricultural work was also valued. Agricultural yield grew as herds multiplied.

During the third millennium, the Egyptians tried to domesticate wild animals of the desert and the marshes, and such easily tamed species as cattle and donkeys shared the pastures, with greater or less success, with antelopes, gazelles, ibex, hyenas, herons, and cranes, all captured in their natural habitats. Some of these beasts were ferocious: to force-feed hyenas, it took several breeders to fetter and immobilize them; and the beaks of cranes had to be tied to their necks when the force-feeding was done. All these attempts at domestication were unsuccessful and progressively abandoned toward the end of the third millennium. The Egyptians then devoted themselves exclusively to the raising of bovines and ovines, and in the representations of processions of animals, we see essentially bulls, cows, donkeys, sheep, goats, rams, and more rarely, pigs. The horse would not arrive in Egypt until around 1600 B.C.E., after the invasion by the Hyksos.

The pasture areas were the marshes and swamps, those near the river or the canals and also those in the delta, where the grass growing in abundance supplied considerable forage. The delta was the place inhabited by cowherds, shepherds, and their animals. Like the peasants, they worked on behalf of great estates, which in their turn were accountable to Pharaoh's government for the condition of their herds. As a social group, herdsmen were clearly distinguished by their marginality; living in the marshes, they were more familiar with this aquatic world than with the human environment. Leading a seminomadic life, the herdsman went from pasture to pasture, accompanied by his dog, and with the mat on which he stretched out at night rolled up on his shoulder. He sometimes took shelter in a hut made of rushes to prepare his snack and roast a bird on his campfire. In the reliefs in mastabas, he can easily be recognized by his shaved or bald head and his ill-shaven jowls. As he usually waded through the water along with his animals, he went naked, carefully carrying his loincloth, his mat, his food, some cooking utensils, and a stick on his shoulder. To relieve his solitude, he talked to his animals, giving them affectionate nicknames: "Hey, Treasure, eat your bread," says a herdsman cajolingly to his ox. He also knew the good spots where the meadow was well watered and the grass was high, and he would lead his herd there, carrying in his arms the calves still too small to walk in the deep water of the canal (Figure 29). This fording was always dangerous, for crocodiles lay in wait for the approaching animals, ready to devour the youngest ones.

The herdsman played an active role in the mating process and in the delivery of the newborn calf. He selected the best bull for breeding, and then, at calving time, he delivered his cow with an expert hand. Seeing that an interested bull has strayed a bit too close to his cow, one herdsman exclaims, "Hey, guardian! Don't let that bull mount her!" In another scene, in which the wide-eyed cow, tongue hanging out, is writhing this way and that, ready to calve, we read, "Pull hard, guardian, she's in pain!" Milking the cows was an everyday task of the herdsmen; to make it easier, they fettered the animals' hind legs and sat under their bellies, causing an abundant stream of milk to flow into a jar. The cow dung was salvaged by the children of the surrounding villages. Collecting it in baskets that they placed on their heads, they carried it back to their mothers, who set it out to dry in the sun and thus obtained an excellent fuel for their cooking needs.

FIGURE 29.
Herdsmen and cattle fording a canal. From the mastaba of Princess Idut at
Saqqara. Photo by Guillemette Andreu.

CATTLE COUNTS AND BUTCHERING

The apparent freedom of the shepherds and cowherds had its limits. Every two years during the Old Kingdom, and then each year at the end of the Sixth Dynasty (c. 2200 B.C.E.), they had to submit to the burdensome ceremony of the cattle count organized by the administration that managed the estate to which the animals belonged. The lord and master personally attended the proceedings, which saw the participation of all the scribes of the domain, along with the overseers and other intendants charged with drawing up the accounts. This was the occasion for verifying the number of head of each species, registering births, and handing out compliments or punishments as results warranted. All the flocks and herds of the estate were marched in close ranks under the eyes of the owner, and the number of animals thus inspected was recorded. In the Giza tomb of Khaefra-ankh of the Fifth Dynasty (c. 2500 B.C.E.), the owner records 834 head of longhorned cattle, 220 head of cattle without horns, 2,234 goats, 760 donkeys,

FIGURE 30.
Cattle being butchered. After The Sakkarah Expedition, The Mastaba of Mereruka, *The University of Chicago Oriental Institute Publications 31 (Chicago: The University of Chicago Press, 1938), Part II, Plate 109. Courtesy of The Oriental Institute of The University of Chicago.*

and 974 sheep. The registration was carried out by scribes sitting cross-legged next to a small table bearing their writing equipment. One by one, each manager of a portion of the estate was led to this "office" by a well-muscled escort; he had to declare his figure and submit to a beating if it was deemed too low. The same fiscal police worked at both the harvest accounts and the cattle counts; armed with truncheons, they punished the bad payers and pursued the cheaters. Their ranks swelled in the Middle Kingdom, and we find them serving as police and providing security in the ranks of mining expeditions.

Once counted, the cattle were divided into two groups, those returning to pasture and those to be led to slaughter. It could happen that an animal, arriving at the threshold of the slaughterhouse, reared up and then stood transfixed on the ground: "Pull hard! Push her! Hold on to her!" a drover cries out to his assistants. In the slaughterhouse, under the expert eye of a veterinarian and a group of priests who would receive a part of the meat for funerary offerings, the animal was trussed up and turned on its back, and its throat was slit before it was cut up. When a steer or bull is represented,

FIGURE 31.

Bottom register: birds being fed; left and center, fenced enclosures with central basins. Top register: force-feeding of birds; across the upper portion of the register, the various species of birds are allowed to take a "promenade" after their meal. After Lucienne Épron, François Daumas, Georges Goyon, and Pierre Montet, Le Tombeau de Ti, Mémoires publiés par les membres de l'Institut Français d'Archéologie Orientale du Caire 65, fascicle 1 (Cairo: Institut Français d'Archéologie Orientale du Caire, 1939), Plate VI. © IFAO. Reproduced by permission of the Institut Français d'archéologie Orientale du Caire.

it seems enormous in proportion to its butcher (Figure 30). The ritual butchering began with the severing of a front hoof and then a rear one, followed by the removal of the heart and the other internal organs. The butchers worked in pairs, with the help of assistants who held the limbs to be cut off, collected the blood of the victim, and carried off the quarters of meat as they were removed. A head butcher exclaims, "Hurry, comrades, the ceremony has begun! Carry these ribs to the table before the master of ceremonies arrives!" To one, he says, "There's a section of ribs to be taken — hurry!"

THE POULTRY YARD

Mainly geese and ducks were raised in the poultry yards. So many other water fowl were taken in the marshes on hunting parties that it seemed useless to burden the farms with birds that could be obtained so easily. Chickens did not appear until the middle of the fifteenth century, when Tuthmosis III marveled at this animal that laid an egg per day! On the great farms of the Old Kingdom, there were constructions devoted to aviculture, with a central basin and channels (Figure 31). In general, the birds were raised in the open air and enjoyed a certain freedom. But force-feeding could be practiced by sturdy, strapping men who firmly clutched the animals to make them to eat. After this meal taken under duress, the birds were allowed to stretch their legs in the enclosure of the building: "Promenade of the ducks and white geese after their meal," we read above a scene on a wall of the mastaba of Ty (c. 2400 B.C.E.). Their walk was a short one, and they were quickly returned to the shed, which was shut up with wire netting.

APICULTURE

Scenes of beekeeping rarely occur in the tombs of ancient Egypt, but mentions of honey and the presence of the bee in the hieroglyphic script are so widespread that we can conclude there was a well-organized apiculture as early as the Old Kingdom, as is otherwise attested in a relief in the sun temple of King Neuserre (2485–2470 B.C.E.) at Abusir. The prerogative of royal meals in this period, the use of honey expanded in the Middle Kingdom, to pastry making, perfumery, and medicinal products. At the site of Gebelein, the French Egyptologist Gaston-Camille-Charles Maspero discovered pots and cakes of honey in tombs of the Eleventh Dynasty (c. 2000 B.C.E.). Apiaries were made of cylindrical pots arranged horizontally, one row on top of another. The harvest took place at the end of autumn: the apiary was smoked in order to remove the honeycomb, which the beekeepers then decanted into large, spherical jars that they sealed hermetically.

In Egyptian mythology, humankind, animals, and plant life all sprang from the same creative act of the creator god and were intended by nature to participate, peacefully and in harmony, in the smooth operation of the world. For the Egyptians, all this living world was animated by the same concern for enforcing Maat, the cosmic order and equilibrium instituted by the creator. From the beginning of history on, a good relationship was spontaneously established between people and their animals, and theological systems attributed many animal forms to the deities. Even today, this physical symbiosis of river, human, and animal is one of the most striking traits of Egyptian civilization.

9 FISHING AND HUNTING

A major element of the ancient Egyptian landscape — one lost in our modern visions of the land — was its overgrown areas, dense and luxuriant with thickets of papyrus. Besides the fields and gardens devoted to systematic agricultural exploitation, there were dead river branches and, especially, vast swampy areas, where the stagnant water favored superabundant growth of reeds and papyrus. These swampy depressions, called "lowlands" in the texts, were mostly in the delta, but they are mentioned here and there in the provinces of the valley. They were an ideal preserve for fishing and for hunting water fowl but also the refuge of hippopotamuses and crocodiles, which had to be avoided, or better, hunted, on outings into these territories.

For the Egyptians, an especially good time was to be had on the occasional day spent in the marshes, fishing and hunting in the company of family and friends. The best season was at the end of the inundation, when the migratory birds were ready to depart. Notwithstanding the threat of hippopotamuses and crocodiles, this was a charming locale, where they loved to glide soundlessly in light skiffs between the papyrus plants, with their graceful umbels, and the sweetly perfumed water lilies, to breathe the fresh air and admire the sunlight the whole day long, to let the children bathe when it was warm, and to make a good catch or simply marvel at the din and liveliness of all the animals abounding in this watery jungle. Frogs, grasshoppers, butterflies and dragonflies, swarms of kingfishers in flight, ibis, herons, lapwings, pigeons, fledglings piping in their nests, weasels climbing on a stalk of papyrus, mongooses: all these are represented in this marshy landscape, which is especially well illustrated by scenes in mastabas of the Old King-

FIGURE 32.

Fowling with the boomerang. From a Middle Kingdom tomb at Beni Hasan. After C. R. Lepsius, Denkmaeler aus Aegypten und Aethiopien *(Berlin: Nicolai, 1849–56), Plate 130.*

dom. The Egyptians did in fact want to take images of their happiness in this life with them into the hereafter, and the impressive number of carved scenes in their tombs depicting their activities in the marshes indicates how choice an occasion this was during a lifetime on earth.

HUNTING

Hunting with the boomerang (Figure 32), which was combined with harpoon fishing, was apparently a prerogative reserved for the privileged of this world — the royal family, courtiers, and important persons in the administration. Such outings are presented as occasions of sportive amusement in which the skills of the ruling class were highlighted. As he stands in his boat of bound papyrus stalks, the tomb owner's ability excites the admiration of his wife and children, who sit affectionately at his feet, occupy-

FIGURE 33.

Trapping birds. From an Old Kingdom mastaba at Saqqara. After C. R. Lepsius,
Denkmaeler aus Aegypten und Aethiopien *(Berlin: Nicolai, 1849–56), Plate 46.*

ing themselves with picking water lilies or collecting the birds he has
caught. With a sure motion, he throws the boomerang at the birds and
recovers his weapon after felling two or three unfortunate fowl in their
flight. A religious text of the Middle Kingdom exalts these exploits with the
boomerang: "You pick the lotuses and the flowers, and the water fowl come
to you. You throw your boomerang at them, and they fall at the whistling
of its sound." We then read a list of the birds thus caught: ducks, cranes,
snipes, geese, plovers, quail, and so forth.

Hunting with a boomerang, so gratifying for its hero, nevertheless did
not offer a very good return. To increase the yield, the bird hunters developed a rather effective trap operated by a team of five or six men under the
direction of a leader (Figure 33). The men choose a flat area with a pond in
its center and fasten, on opposite sides of the water surface, a net with two
movable parts, controlled by a long maneuvering rope. Some grains of
wheat and some worms serve as bait, while tame birds, the hunters' accom-
plices, are set loose near the pond. With something to eat and drink, the
place seems like a paradise, and birds soon flock, heedless of the trap awaiting them. Not a man is in sight, the hunters hidden behind a bush a short
distance from the pond. For complete freedom of movement, they have
taken off their loincloths, which we sometimes see rolled up on a mat near
the scene. The leader has difficulty maintaining silence: "There's a flock of
birds in arm's reach, hunter, if you keep quiet," we read above a scene of
hunting with the net. The leader holds a strip of cloth in his hand, and as
soon as he thinks there are enough birds on the pond, he waves it. That is
the signal. The hunters give the rope a hard pull and nimbly draw the net
over their game: "Pull, comrade, it's full of birds for you!" The following
scene shows the bird hunters getting back up, after the force of their effort
has sent them sprawling on the ground. They must quickly remove the
stunned birds from the net; beginning with those still strong enough to es-

cape and then disentangling those stuck in the mesh. To immobilize the birds, they cross the wings of each one and set it on the ground. Meanwhile, two of the hunters fold up the net and pack the birds into crates. "The cage is full," says one of the men, satisfied, in front of a stuffed crate. Such hunting parties were always quite lively and joyous, and we sense that the young men enjoyed their sporting exploit and their well-coordinated teamwork.

Children did not go alone into the marshes, where too many menacing denizens lay in wait for them. They had to content themselves with the small fowl of the fields to bring home something to add to the daily bread. They would go in bands and set traps to catch the crows, quail, pigeons, lapwings, swallows, hoopoes, and orioles that were attracted by the ripe ears of grain, to the great displeasure of the cultivators. The trap illustrated in a tomb of the Middle Kingdom at Beni Hasan is simple, but it has a functional mechanical device: it is a small net mounted in a flexible wooden frame and activated by a spring. A worm was placed in it, and as the bird approached, its beating wings hit a cord that released the spring and closed the net over the animal. One had only to collect the bird, put the trap back in place, and await the next victim. The young hunter remained close to his trap, hidden in the wheat. He himself acted as decoy, imitating the bird's call with his voice.

FISH FOR ALL TASTES

There were innumerable fishing grounds in ancient Egypt. Besides the marshes and the swamps, which were particularly well stocked, one could fish in the Nile itself, in the canals, and perhaps also on the coast of the Mediterranean or the Red Sea, though no mention is made of such activity in these areas in the age of the pyramids: the frail boats were not made for such deep waters or such strong currents.

Like hunting, fishing was both an occasion for a family outing in the country for the nobility and a full time job for professional fishermen. It could be done all year long in the marshy areas or the Nile, and nearly all species of fish were edible. In the bas-reliefs of Ty (c. 2400 B.C.E.), we recognize mullet, perch, eel, carp, tench, cichlid (also called bulti), different varieties of oxyrhynchus, catfish, and the Nile tetrodon, also called sea urchin. A French zoologist has distinguished as many as twenty-four species, still known today.

Fish was a delicacy much appreciated by the Egyptians, who consumed much more of it than red meat, and they ate it raw, dried, or pickled. Today

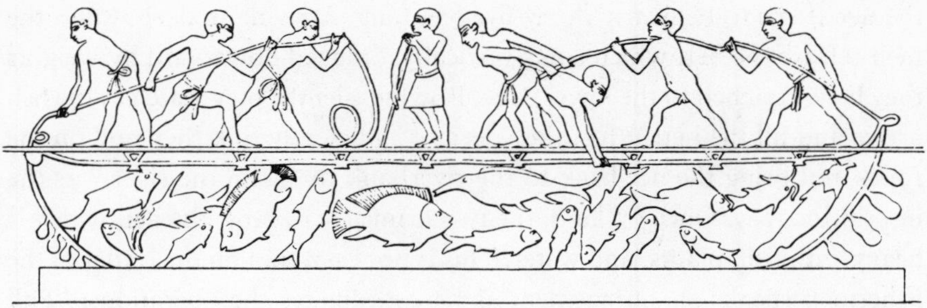

FIGURE 34.
Fishing with a seine. From an Old Kingdom mastaba at Giza. After C. R. Lepsius,
Denkmaeler aus Aegypten und Aethiopien *(Berlin: Nicolai, 1849–56), Plate 9.*

they are still quite fond of a preparation of more or less decomposed, salted fish that, it is agreed, goes back to the pharaonic era. As for botargo, a kind of caviar made of pressed, dried, and salted mullet eggs, we see from several reliefs in mastabas that it was made on the fishing grounds themselves. A religious taboo, however, forbade temple personnel from consuming fish and advised ordinary mortals to abstain from eating it before entering a sanctuary. Every species of fish, like every animal otherwise, was in fact thought to be the avatar of a known deity of the Egyptian pantheon, who could at any moment manifest himself in another form and express his wrath. But these considerations in fact affected only a tiny part of a population that otherwise loved to eat the fish the gods were pleased to create in their waters.

Like the peasants and the bird hunters, the fishermen were part of the permanent personnel of a great estate managed by an important personage chosen by Pharaoh's government from the royal family or the local notables to administer its economy. And like the other personnel, they were ordinary people who worked in teams and received as wages a ration from the yield of their catch. Nothing distinguished the fisherman: like the cowherd, he went naked, carrying his loincloth wrapped around his shoulder.

FISHING

Techniques for catching fish were developed quite early. Some of them were undoubtedly already known in the prehistoric period and scarcely changed with time. Fishing with a seine (Figure 34) was the most productive method: on two boats, two teams hold a large net by a cable from on board each boat, carrying it far from the bank. On a wall of the mastaba of Ty, the net seems to be nearly thirty-five feet long. Arriving in deep water, the men release the net, which sinks vertically, dragged downward by weights they have attached to the lower edge. Rowing silently, they watch as the fish arrive and fill the net. When they deem it sufficiently full, they pull on the ropes and bring the net back to the riverbank to "skim the river," as the inscriptions say. Once on land, the two teams try to hoist the net, which is heavy with fish, plants, and water. This is not easy, though the leader of the fishermen speaks encouragement as he coordinates the operations: "Pull hard, it's a beautiful day! Look, look, the fish are magnificent!" or again, "What a fisherman, what a net!" The load is sometimes so heavy that they need the help of a strap to pull it, putting their shoulders into the effort; but the strap wounds their skin, and pain can be read on their faces.

Fishing with a keepnet was commonly practiced; it demanded less effort, but its yield was inferior. Its advantage was that one could do without a boat: it sufficed to know how to swim. Made of wickerwork, the net had the appearance of a bottle, one part of which was shaped like a neck; it was rather like the principle of the pot used by present-day fishermen. A stopper or a sliding knot was positioned at the neck end, while the other end was blocked by a curtain of pliant stalks that allowed the fish to pass through and then closed up behind them. The fishermen slipped bait into the trap and placed it in the water, after attaching a float to serve as a marker when they collected the pots. They went in pairs to collect the keepnets, hoping to find them so full that one man would not suffice. But the conversation between the two partners could turn sour: "Hold on to the net, comrade, or else your goods will go into someone else's belly!" "Is it you who are telling me what to do, thief?" Sometimes, the setting of the nets took place in deep water and by boat: "Pull hard on the oars so that we arrive above it!" And there was the cry of satisfaction: "Filled to the brim! This time, it's a success!" The happy fishermen empty the contents of their basket directly onto the bottom of the boat and immediately throw the net back into the water. One of them has found in the catch a redoubtable catfish, with its poisonous backbone; swiftly, he removes it.

Fishing with a landing net and with a line were practiced alone. Generally represented together, these types of fishing seem to be spare-time activities of the marsh men; not far from them, their comrades are busy harvesting papyrus and rushes and making nets and boats. The net used resembled that still seen today: it was made of a triangular wooden frame, to which a deep net was attached. The fisherman sat in a little papyrus boat, or remained on the bank in the shade of a tree. Silence and patience were in order, as in angling. In the latter, the fisherman, seated in a boat, dropped a line, with hook and bait, into the water. He knew he might have to wait a long time and took the precaution of bringing food, placed in a basket at his feet; his snack consisted of bread with a little something on it, a flat cake, and a jug of beer. As soon as he sensed that he had a catch, he pulled out the line and struck the fish with the swift blow of a mallet.

Once the catch was in, the men were occupied with processing the fish. Depending on the distance separating the fishing grounds from the estate, the fish were treated either still on board the boat or after arrival on land. Because the greater part of the catch's yield was not intended for immediate consumption, the fish had to be quickly slit, gutted, and set out to dry before piling them, already hardened, into well-ventilated crates.

One of the pleasures of fishing expeditions was the moment of return, at nightfall. To the joyous tumult of the birds were added the shouts of the watermen as they gave vent to their satisfaction with their productive day. The temperature falls, a breeze refreshes the air, and a good mood comes over the hearts of the men. On the canals, the boats follow one another, or they pass and even graze one another. The men shout from one boat to another and try to seize the fish from neighboring boats, and this game leads to a real battle. They stand up and with blows of their sticks, they try to knock one another into the water or to overturn their adversaries' boat. Shouts ring out: "Get even with him! Trip him up!" A collective bath generally followed, bringing to an end a nearly ritual game that had just concluded a good day's fishing.

HIPPOPOTAMUS HUNTING

We have seen that the great threat hanging over all activities in the marshes came from the two ferocious animals they harbored: the crocodile and the hippopotamus. There is no scene of crocodile hunting, though the animal is widely represented in the reliefs of the mastabas. We see it voracious and ready to gobble a baby hippopotamus as it emerges from its mother's womb, or at home in the waters of the canals with the animals it devours. In the Egyptian pantheon, the crocodile is called "Sobek" and appears as the uncontested lord of the aquatic realm. Fearing the god and in dread of the animal, the Egyptians gave it a wide berth but did not kill it. It was different with the hippopotamus, a dangerous animal assimilated to the negative forces of the world and dedicated to Seth, the god of Evil. Its killing stemmed from the ritual magic performed by the earliest kings of Egypt,

FIGURE 35.

Hippopotamus hunting. After The Sakkarah Expedition, The Mastaba of Mereruka, *The University of Chicago Oriental Institute Publications 31 (Chicago: The University of Chicago Press, 1938), Part I, Plate 13. Courtesy of The Oriental Institute of The University of Chicago.*

who, in harpooning the monster, recalled the victory of the goodly Horus over his maleficent brother Seth.

Hippopotamus hunting is often represented on the walls of the mastabas of the important personages of this world (Figure 35). Prudently, the tomb owner witnesses its capture from the riverbank. Standing in their boats, the harpooners locate a group of hippopotamuses and pursue it, trying to contain one of them in an especially dense thicket of papyrus. Their weapon is a harpoon, attached to a rope and provided with hooks that sink like banderillas into the mouth of the animal, cruelly wounding it. The men grip the ropes, and when they reckon that the animal is sufficiently hurt and weakened, they pull on it to draw it to the bank. Once it is hauled onto land, the hippopotamus is finished off and cut to pieces.

The harpoon also had a less violent use, that of catching fish venturing close to the boats of the tomb owners, who alternately speared fish and hunted with the boomerang during their family outings. The children take their places in the prow of the boat and point out the spots teeming with fish; the tomb owner then stands and harpoons several fish with a single

FIGURE 36.
Middle register, left: papyrus harvester chewing on a stalk of papyrus; right: cattle mating. Above: boats made of papyrus. Below: herdsman driving cattle. From an Old Kingdom mastaba, originally in Saqqara. © Chuzeville. Photo courtesy of The Louvre.

stroke. The catch is so good that a column of water shoots up in front of the boat, rising as high as the fisherman. All the company cry out, and the wife, moved, puts an arm around the leg of her hero.

WORK IN THE MARSHES

When not taken up with fishing or hunting, the men of the marshes were quite usefully occupied with the last major activity that took place in this swampy land: the gathering of papyrus, the collecting of water lilies, and the harvesting of reeds. With the papyrus and the reeds, they could make or repair their work tools, and we see their expert hands manufacturing ropes, mats, baskets, huts, even light boats. Part of the papyrus harvest went to the domain to be transformed into writing material for the work of the scribes; another part was kept for immediate consumption as food. Egyptians in fact loved to chew a piece of papyrus stalk (Figure 36), sucking its sap, somewhat as they do today in the countryside with pieces of sugarcane. Papyrus was pulled up when its stalk had reached a height rather greater than that of a man. The work is easy, and it is practically a recreational activity that passes quite pleasantly under the supervision of a leader. A worker may take advantage of the opportunity to gather some water lilies, much appreciated for their perfume and their beautiful white petals. Very quickly, the papyrus stalks are gathered and taken to the workshop. But the bundles are long and heavy, so the men who carry them on their backs walk with difficulty, bent over. One of them loses his balance, and his comrades help him: "Get up!" "Yes, sir!"

Once set on the ground, the bundles of papyrus are untied, and work begins on the stalks. The first operation is the removal, from the stalks, of the fibers, which are to be the raw material of manufactured items. The goal is to obtain fibers of equal length, which are then cleaned before being consigned to two people who plait them. The shorter plaits are used to make baskets, mats, or seats; the longer ones reserved for the boatyards, for making the light boats so useful for work in the marshes. The boatbuilders set to work in a flat, shady area quite close to the canals, which allows them to try out their boats. The curved hull was made of bundles of supple stalks, which were given a permanent contour by fastening them to a frame. The stalks, bundled compactly together, were attached to one another by crosspieces of pliant wood fastened in place with ropes. Each rope could be wound around the hull as many as three times, thus assuring that no crevice could remain under such tension. This was highly skilled labor, and children were present to lend an occasional hand: "Hey, little one, bring us some ropes!" "Right away, father, take this rope," a lad says, admiring the boat his father is busy making. There was no need for an overseer to direct the manufacture of papyrus boats; for the men knew and loved their work well. It made for an entertaining sight, and the owner of the domain did not disdain to tour the boatyard, while the old workmen who no longer had the strength to pull on the ropes came to chat with the teams and give them some advice.

HUNTING IN THE DESERT

The climatic and ecological changes in Egypt in the course of the third millennium considerably modified the habitats of the larger game, driving the animals considered wild out of the valley, deep into the desert. Consequently the hunting ground became the "red land," which in the vocabulary of the hieroglyphic texts designates the desert, the uninhabited and deadly world frequented by the god Seth, the brother who betrayed Horus, the mythical first king of Egypt. The ideogram for the desert, which represents three mountains of sand separated by two passes, is used as a determinative in writing words for hostile geographic notions associated with it: cemetery, desert, foreign lands. Its color is russet red, like that of the hair of enemies or, again, of a form of the god Seth.

Thus it was not for pleasure that the Egyptian people left the pleasant banks of the Nile to venture into these distant regions. Only need prompted them, when they had to bag game for the great tables of the valley or extract minerals from the quarries. Nevertheless, dangerous though it was, hunting in the desert was also an opportunity to display courage. The king and his courtiers risked it, and it even became one of their favorite pastimes, an elite sport recounted on the walls of their tombs.

Thanks to these illustrated descriptions, it is easy to reconstruct the setting of the desert hunt. On a sandy, rolling terrain dotted here and there with thorny bushes and scrub, the animals of the desert peacefully devote themselves to the pleasures of their existence. A gazelle nurses her little one, while its young father, concerned for its comfort, digs a little hole in the sand for it to rest its chin while taking a siesta. Some yards away, a jerboa enters its den, and a hare is on the lookout behind a grove, while a hedgehog wanders in search of insects. Elsewhere, wolves and panthers mate, while a wild she-ass gives birth under the greedy eye of a golden fox. Gazelles frisk about between the dunes, letting flocks of ostriches and herds of bubalises pass by. A giraffe walks with slow step, as a swift deer slips between its legs. Still further away, a lion and a wild bull engage in merciless combat; a leopard is in flight.

DESERT SPECIALISTS

When they went in search of this game, princes and peasants engaged *nuu*, hunters specializing in these regions. Seminomadic and living on the margins of the valley, these professionals knew by heart the desert sands and the rocky grounds from which they fearlessly flushed out any living thing lying in wait. Moreover, it was to them that the state turned when it needed to prospect for new quarries or conduct a manhunt to bring back fugitives escaped from work camps in the valley. They were principally employed to assure the success of hunts in the desert, and they spent their time roaming the trails, tracking antelopes, oryxes, ostriches, wild asses, gazelles, hyenas, ibex, wolves, wild sheep, wild goats, deer, and wild bulls. They set out on expedition armed with various weapons, which they would choose expertly according to the animal they were tracking. These weapons were long staffs, boomerangs, lassos, and of course, bows and arrows. But their most reliable and faithful accessory was undoubtedly their greyhound, which can be recognized by its long legs, long muzzle, upright ears, and curled tail. The relationship between the hunter and his dog was so close that it was not uncommon for professional hunters to have themselves represented in the company of their dogs, whose names were carved under their images, on the funerary stelae designed to decorate their tombs. Tame hyenas could also accompany expeditions to the desert. Their strong, unpleasant scent covered that of the men, hiding the arrival of the hunters from the game, thus enabling the men to capture the animals, which were cut short in their attempt to flee. The hunt over, we see the leader of the group, holding his four dogs and his two hyenas by the leash; they are followed unenthusiastically by a puppy and a young hyena, which have just experienced their first training in assisting the hunt.

The hunt began when, having penetrated deep into the desert, the men released their dogs and hyenas. Their hope was to bring the greatest possible number of game animals back alive for domestication. The best technique was to lasso them, which impeded the animals without wounding them. But the dogs go ahead of them and attack as many animals as they can catch; here they massacre antelopes, and there they bite the paws of young oryxes, while a wild goat stumbles as it tries to flee. The men follow and shoot at the animals that the greyhounds have not stopped.

Sometimes, to be sure of bringing back many animals, hunting with a net was practiced. The principle was somewhat the same as that for netting game fish: it was a matter of luring the animals into a trap that had the appearance of a pleasant, peaceful spot (Figure 37). A slightly depressed area was chosen and surrounded by a continuous net broken by a single potential point of access. The spot was attractive, with food and water placed at the center. Gradually, the animals entered in large numbers, feeding and enjoying themselves in this spot that seemed in every way ideal. When the enclosure was filled with game, the hunters quickly closed the entrance and released their dogs to contain the animals. Some arrows, skillfully shot, soon ended the rebellion of the captured animals. Dust flew, wounded animals railed, the dogs barked, the noise was deafening. The legend of a scene of hunting with a net, painted in a tomb at Deir el-Bersha at the end of the third millennium B.C.E., is eloquent regarding the result:

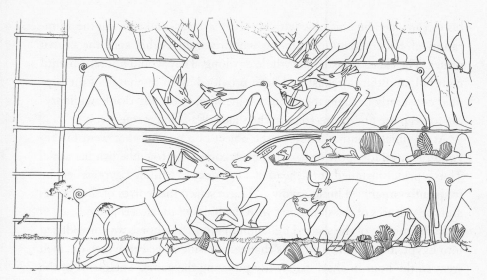

FIGURE 37.
Hunting within an enclosure (note a portion of the enclosure on the left). After
The Sakkarah Expedition, The Mastaba of Mereruka, *The University of Chicago*
Oriental Institute Publications 31 (Chicago: The University of Chicago Press,
1938), Part I, Plate 25. Courtesy of The Oriental Institute of The University of
Chicago.

"Watching the capture of the antelopes of the desert. There are a great many
of them, more than all inside the net."

Then thoughts could turn to going home to the valley. The vizier Ptahhotpe had the return of the hunters, bearing their trophies, carved in his
tomb. The leader brings up the rear of the troop. In front of him proceeds a
man conveying two cages, in which we recognize hares and jerboas; another
man shoulders a gazelle; a third is carrying young antelopes and the rem-
nants of the day's picnic, composed of bread and beer. But the most beautiful trophies are caged. A lion and a panther, behind bars, are drawn on
sledges by four men walking backward, afraid to relax their vigilance: the
cage is of wood, and it would take little effort for the captive animals to
break the bars.

When hunting was practiced as an elite sport by the royal family and
their courtiers, it was more a matter of a courageous exercise than a food-
procuring chore. If it was Pharaoh leading a safari in person, his task was
greatly facilitated for him. When he and his retinue arrived at the locale of
his exploits, the game had already been driven into the enclosure. His servants respectfully handed him arrow after arrow, which he adroitly shot at

his victims, bending his bow with his great strength and exciting the admiration of his companions, among whom would be his son, the crown prince. The exercise lasted the whole day long. They would not return until nightfall, and thus a repast had been provided. Men in charge of the supplies constantly brought the hunters something to eat and drink, while trying to keep the provisions fresh in the shade of a solitary tree.

At all times, hunting could be the object of a passion that went far beyond the need for sport or to bring back something to embellish the table. Thus a prince installed at the head of a province of Middle Egypt, where he frequently organized hunts, avows, "I have seized the wolves of the deserts and the vultures of the sky, along with the hides of the desert game."

In the middle of the second millennium B.C.E., the horse was introduced into Egypt, and hunting methods changed considerably. From then on, men went to the hunt in chariots, swiftly pursuing the game. The farms of the valley raised enough livestock to feed the population, and the capture of desert game became a luxurious pastime, much prized by the sovereigns.

10 A PEOPLE OF BELIEVERS

The immanence of the divine in Egyptian thought was a characteristic trait of pharaonic civilization. We can, for example, find striking proof in the lists of personal names borne by Nile valley inhabitants from the dawn of history on, which have been patiently collected by Egyptologists of the twentieth century. In their books, we note an overwhelming majority of theophoric names that place children born on the banks of the Nile under the protection of one of the deities of the Egyptian pantheon and reveal the close ties uniting the world of the living with that of their religious imagination.

THE EVOLUTION OF RELIGIOUS THOUGHT

The origin of the world, the existence and functions of the gods, and life after death are mysterious and universal questions to which the ancient Egyptians tried to furnish answers. It is undoubtedly in the domain of religious thought, cultic practices, and beliefs that Egyptologists perceive the most development and the deepest changes in the course of the three millennia of the existence of pharaonic Egypt. Gods unknown or minor in the Old Kingdom, such as Osiris or Amun, would experience a brilliant destiny in later periods and come to occupy the largest temples in the nation. As important a religious concept as a royal tomb in the form of a pyramid whose imposing mass obstructed the flat horizon of the desert would disappear in favor of rock cut tombs hidden in the secret recesses of the Valley of the Kings, causing the barque of the deceased king to leave the company of the heavenly bodies and navigate through the realm of the netherworld. The animal cults, so striking to ancient Greek travelers, are scarcely mentioned in the texts and temples of the third millennium. The priestly class, which was ubiquitous in Late Period Egyptian society, nowhere appears as a specialized group distinct from others in the Old Kingdom. We could easily multiply examples of this evolution, which even took on the pace of a revolution in the fourteenth century B.C.E. with the institution of the exclusive cult of the sun disk imposed by the pharaoh Amenophis IV (later: Akhenaten). To these historical and chronological reforms can be added another, purely documentary factor that complicates our analysis of Egyptian religion in the age of the pyramids. Contemporary sources on the subject are especially poor: for the Old Kingdom, only the funerary beliefs relating to the destiny of the king are fairly well known, thanks to the texts covering the chambers of the pyramids beginning with the end of the Fifth Dynasty. The documentation changes and becomes somewhat more diversified in the Middle Kingdom, so that we can discern the cults and concepts of the Egyptians of that period. But there again, it is more a matter of funerary beliefs and of practices related to the afterlife than of everyday piety in sanctuaries consecrated to local deities. The paucity of remains of temples to the gods practically forbids any serious reconstruction of the rituals that must have been perpetuated there on a daily basis.

Consequently, it should not be surprising that specialists in Egyptian religion have devoted their labors to analyzing the monuments and texts of later periods, so rich in precious information about the daily cult ritual and the animal cults. From the New Kingdom through the Roman period, archaeologists have well preserved temples, both divine and funerary, at their disposal, and philologists can draw on the columns of hieroglyphs of monumental inscriptions and illustrated papyri for the explication of the world made by the writers of the sacred Egyptian texts. To understand the festivals and ceremonies that took place in an Egyptian temple, the visitor can find no better spot than the temple of Dendara, though it was constructed in an Egypt dominated by Greeks and Romans. But historians of the age of the pyramids, knowing what changes occurred in thought and concepts, cannot extrapolate the most ancient beliefs and practices from the religious imagery of the temple of Dendara, which was decorated nearly twenty-five hundred years after the period in which they are interested.

UNCHANGING BELIEFS

Nevertheless, there were constants, beliefs that sprung up at the beginning of the third millennium and persisted through the centuries, permanently underlying the attitude of the Egyptians toward their gods. The explanation of the birth of the world was one of these lasting concepts, and it was accompanied by a major, enduring concern: the end of the world, or more precisely, the return to the original chaos, to the state that had preceded the creation of the universe.

In the beginning was Nun, a liquid, undifferentiated expanse, the dark, primordial ocean from which the first piece of land emerged by the will of the self-actualized creator god. Thanks to the creator of the "first moment," light appeared and the world was born, bringing with it humankind, plants, the river, the seasons, and all of nature's miracles. He also created the gods, vital forces dispersed through the world to assure its proper functioning. Each deity was an emanation of the creator, who divided and multiplied himself until he produced a sometimes extravagant, polymorphic, and complex pantheon that participated in the cosmic equilibrium. This perfect harmony of the world thus created, in which each thing had its place, was defined by the notion of Maat, which encompassed, at one and the same time, the moral values, the laws of society, and the physical features that conferred its diversity and its order upon the land. Maat ruled the universe, thanks to the daily work of Pharaoh, who was responsible for the cults and rituals that averted the risk of a return to chaos. The fear that the universe might again be swallowed up by the undifferentiated and inert chaos surrounding it occupied the thoughts of the Egyptians because the threat was ever present: night was a time of tragedy for the sun; daytime, an infernal period for the moon and the stars. Every successful completion of a period in the natural, physical world was experienced as a victory over the forces of chaos, which could be repelled but never destroyed. The role of rites and rituals was to stave off the negative and maleficent aspects of the higher powers.

THE ROLE OF THE TEMPLE

A god, being an emanation of the primordial divine energy, thus assumed all his importance from his role in maintaining the order of the universe. To honor him and provide a setting for his lofty role, a temple was built whose material would be stone, more durable and more suitable for carved decoration than the unbaked brick used for houses. From the dawn of history, each locality had its deity, who was endowed with a specific myth and liturgy. As the unification of the Egyptian realm progressed and cultural and cultic contacts were established among the various provinces of the land, religion was enriched by a multitude of opinions and beliefs, none of them excluded. This multiplicity of approaches, with its accumulation of apparently contradictory causes for enduring phenomena, is another of the constant principles of Egyptian religious thought. It is based on the idea that a single aspect cannot suffice to explain the essential nature of the divine, which maintains a singularity of character within the multiplicity of its actions and forms. Thus there were different cosmogonies in the various locales, but they could be combined and made complementary. At Memphis, doctrine made Ptah the creator. He was the "risen land," the ground of the first day, the fashioner of Pharaoh's flesh, and the artisan of all organic matter. At Heliopolis, it was Re-Atum-Khepri, the daily sun, who was the origin of the birth of the world, which he entrusted to his descendants united in the Ennead of Heliopolis. With regard to this solar god, we read in a passage of the Pyramid Texts, "He was born in Nun, when the sky did not yet exist, when the earth did not yet exist, when nothing established yet existed, when even disorder did not yet exist." Finally, at Hermopolis in Middle Egypt, the theologians believed that the act of creation was due to a group of four divine pairs called the Ogdoad, who inseminated a plant or an egg, thus giving birth to the light of the sun. The Egyptians reconciled these diverse concepts and adopted others in the course of the centuries down to the Roman period, without trying to eliminate their contradictions.

The Egyptian pantheon thus took on its polymorphic aspect, multiplying its constituent parts and its deities. As early as the Old Kingdom, names of celebrated deities appear, such as Horus, Isis, Osiris, Hathor, and Min, whose cults were undoubtedly carried out in chapels that today have disappeared. Here and there in the delta and in the Nile valley, traces have been found of cultic buildings devoted to a daily ritual no longer known. In Upper Egypt, at Karnak and in the whole Theban region, archaeological sites have yielded some traces of parts of these temples from the Middle Kingdom, but they were for the most part dismantled by the kings of succeeding reigns and reemployed as building stones in later constructions. After the Old Kingdom, the service of the gods required a specialized personnel acting as delegates of the king, who was the sole being authorized to perform the cult; and that is why offering scenes in temples always set the king face to face with deities in accordance with an immutable rule of exchange of services. The pharaoh, as the intermediary between the human realm and the gods, presents the latter with the offerings necessary for their maintenance: bread, vegetables, beer, wine, milk, incense, and so forth. In return, they accord the king — and consequently his land — life, stability, force, health, and all the qualities needed for the world of Egypt to continue on its course. The act of constructing the temple of Heliopolis, dedicated to the god Atum by Senwosret I of the Twelfth Dynasty, serves as an example to illustrate this principle: "'Behold, my Majesty is thinking of a work that will be remembered . . . in the future as something excellent. I shall erect monuments and set up . . . stelae for Harakhty; for he created me that I might do what he has done and that I might execute what he has commanded. . . . When I come as Horus and take my place and establish offerings for the gods, I shall execute actions in the domain of my father Atum. I shall be vigilant that he become rich, as he will be vigilant that I become his successor. I shall embellish his altars on earth. . . .' These royal companions spoke thus . . . : '. . . Oh sovereign, . . . may your plans be as when the king appears at the Uniting of the Two Lands, when [the surveying cord] is stretched in your temple. . . . You will be great when you erect your monument in Heliopolis, the home of the gods, for your father, the lord of the temple, for Atum.' . . . The king appeared wearing the diadem with two plumes, and all the people were behind him. The chief lector-priest and the scribe of the divine book-roll stretched the surveying cord and untied the knot, and the foundation was laid for this home." The foundation ceremony of this temple, of which nothing remains today at the site of Heliopolis, was the occasion of great popular rejoicing, in which everyone participated. In general, the people were excluded from the sacred precinct of a deity's home and had to wait for extraordinary events of this sort to take part in the rites.

The priests, "servants of the god" appointed for the day-to-day functioning of the temple, were divided into "phylae," or teams, which rotated each month and left a written report of the condition of the premises and the cultic furnishings: "Report of the fourth phyle of the clergy of the temple (of el-Lahun), which is leaving its monthly service. Here is their declaration: All your affairs are in good condition. We have examined all the goods of the temple, and everything belonging to the temple is in good condition for the first phyle . . . , which will take up its monthly service." Within the phyle, we can distinguish the category of *wab* ("pure") priests, who were held to very strict rules of hygiene and cleanliness required for the handling of sacred objects and the ritual slaughter of sacrificial animals. The "Admonitions of Ipuwer," a nostalgic text deploring the decline into which

Egypt had fallen during the First Intermediate Period, complains that cults are no longer being carried out: "Remember the construction of the chapel, the incense poured out in it, the libation water poured from the jar at dawn. Remember the fat birds, the geese and the ducks, and the offerings laid out for the gods. Remember the natron that was chewed (to purify the mouth), the white bread that was prepared. . . . Remember the flagpoles that were raised and the offering tables that were fashioned, while the *wab* priests purified the chapels, (remember) the temple white with plaster as though it were milk, the sweetness of the perfume of the horizon, the richness of the offerings."

ABYDOS AND ITS GOD OSIRIS

In the Middle Kingdom, the cult of Osiris took on the aspect of a national cult, and his religious center, Abydos, became the object of a pilgrimage essential for every Egyptian anxious about the afterlife. The festivals that took place there are well known: by the tens of thousands, Egyptians made the journey to Abydos and celebrated it on their votive monuments, carving in stone the mysteries and spectacles whose theater was the sanctuary of Osiris. Beginning with the Twelfth Dynasty, Osiris, who had been a minor god in the Old Kingdom, became the symbol of resurrection and hope in the hereafter. He incarnated all the possibilities of rebirth: that of the vegetation after the flood and that of life after death. His myth gave reassurance, and beginning with the second millennium, it supplanted those of the other deities of the realm of the dead.

The sacred space at Abydos was continually enlarged by the development of "the temple, the houses, the cities of eternity, the excellent territory of the gods, whose layout surpasses that of every place and over which the god rejoices." A numerous religious and domestic personnel was maintained to organize the Osirian festivals each month. The "terrace of the great god," a vast esplanade associated with the sanctuaries, became the place where the stelae of the pilgrims were erected. Egyptians continued to have themselves buried in their home towns, but to assure the protection of the great god of Abydos, they developed the habit of setting up, in his city, a stela or votive ensemble associating their families and near relatives in a common prayer to Osiris, variants of which are repeated endlessly on these stones: "May the king make an offering to Osiris, lord of Abydos, the great god, that he might grant an offering of bread, beer, cattle, birds, alabaster, clothing, and all good and pure things . . . for the *ka* (soul) of the glorified N, engendered by X, borne by Y." These monuments have been found by the thousands at the site, and our study of them has shown that not all the people named in fact made the journey but that there was a custom of having a friend or a workshop located at Abydos carve such a monument. The modest status of the persons we see figured on the stelae at Abydos is striking: they were policemen, soldiers, guards, lower-ranking scribes, and sometimes hirelings who did not even know the names of their mothers, indicating thus that they were of unknown families. Nevertheless, they had the right to their votive stela at Abydos, a sign of the "democratization" of funerary beliefs in the Middle Kingdom.

The festivals in honor of Osiris were closely followed by the king, who dispatched officials to the sanctuary of the great god to represent him there. In year 19 of the reign of Senwosret III, Ikhernofret, royal seal bearer and favorite of the king, was sent to Abydos to conduct the ceremonies there and to refurbish the cult statue. The text of his stela recounts with considerable vivacity the principal episodes of the Osirian mysteries: "I built the [great], eternal [barque of Osiris]. I made for him a portable reliquary that encloses the perfection of Khentyimentiu, of gold, silver, lapis lazuli, copper, *sesenedjem*-wood, and cedar. I fashioned the gods of his retinue and renewed their reliquaries. I assigned [. . .] the priests to their duties. I taught them the daily cult ritual and the solemn ritual of the beginnings of the seasons. I directed the work on the *neshmet*-barque (the barque shrine of Osiris) and created its shrine. I decorated the breast of the lord of Abydos with lapis lazuli, turquoise, electrum, and all the precious stones required for the decoration of the body of a god. I covered the god with his insignia in my rank of the one in charge of the mysteries, in my function of stolist. I was pure of hand in decorating the god, a *sem*-priest with clean fingers. I conducted the procession of Wepwawet (another funerary deity) when he set out to aid his father. I repelled those who attacked the *neshmet*-barque and overthrew the enemies of Osiris. I conducted the great procession in following the god in his footsteps. I caused the divine barque to travel. . . . I conducted [Osiris . . . lord of] Abydos, into his palace. . . . The purification was carried out and his seat was enlarged." Along the processional route, priests played the roles of the enemies and assistants of the god, until the final victory that assured the survival of the lord of eternity. Huge crowds attended these spectacles, enjoying the portrayal of these mythical battles and deriving from them reasons for belief in the hereafter.

FEAR OF THE HEREAFTER

For the question of human destiny after death was the great affair of the living, who spent their whole lifetimes preparing for it, wavering over the years between serene confidence and doubt. Death was a dramatic episode of existence which no one could recount, though the natural perception of it was that it entailed a loss of the "breath of life." To accept this inevitable end and assist the human mind in envisaging the passage to the realm of the great unknown, the Egyptians invented a whole arsenal of material procedures and magicoreligious ceremonies founded on funerary beliefs that, like other beliefs, underwent some changes but also retained some constants.

The first of these constants was the certainty, mingled with fear, of a divine judgment at death's doorstep. It justified leading an existence in conformity with the spirit of Maat, knowing that every transgression of this moral order willed by the gods would lead inevitably to divine punishment: "When a man arrives (at the riverbank of death), his deeds are placed in a heap beside him, and it is for eternity," recalls the "Instruction for Merykare." This same fear led Egyptians to the incessant repetition of declarations of good conduct on their funerary monuments: "I spoke Maat, I did Maat, I said what is good, I repeated what is good. I attained perfection, for I desired that it be well with people. I judged two men so that they were satisfied. I saved the wretched from the hand of the powerful in that over which I had authority. I gave bread to the hungry, clothing to the naked, a landing to the boatless, a coffin to the one who had no son. I made a boat for him who did not have one. I respected my father, I had the affection of my mother, I raised their children."

CONSTRUCTING A TOMB TO GUARANTEE ETERNITY

Another unchanging trait of the funerary religion, one that appeared as early as the Old Kingdom, was the large scale of the material and the magical means that were developed to guarantee survival. The foremost example of material display was the construction of a tomb, the home of the dead. Cemeteries were located at the edge of the western desert, thus assimilating the journey of the soul of the deceased to that of the setting sun. Built for eternity, these tombs were constructed of large stone blocks or dug into cliffs; many would withstand the ravages of the centuries, thus enabling them to communicate the customs of their ancient owners to modern archaeologists. An Egyptian tomb had two parts, corresponding to two functions. Its subterranean chamber, dug deep into the ground and accessible by a shaft, received the burial of the deceased and his funerary equipment. The chapel in the superstructure was the contact point between the living and the dead, a public place for priests and family to carry out the funerary cult, or quite simply, to gather. Expressed at all times was the fear that the tomb might be visited or violated by a dishonest trespasser, along with threats of vengeance in the hereafter: "Whoever will damage any stone or any brick in this tomb of mine, I shall seize his neck like a bird, and I shall place the terror I inspire in him so well that all the living on earth and the spirits will see him and be afraid." "Oh, you living who are on earth who will pass by this tomb, if you desire that your king reward you and that you obtain the condition of *imakhu* (glorified one) with the great god, do not enter this tomb of mine in a state of impurity. Whoever will enter there in a state of impurity after these words, I shall be judged with him by the great god, and I shall crush his family on earth and their houses with [. . .]."

The construction of a tomb, with its scenes and inscriptions, was not, alas, within the means of everyone. The cemeteries of the courtiers have preserved the remains of the most beautiful tombs, such as the mastabas of Giza and Saqqara, which today we visit enraptured. But the eternal homes of ordinary people were more modest. The Sixth Dynasty cemetery of Balat in el-Dakhla Oasis contains, side by side with the immense mastabas of the governors of the oasis, very crude burials, simple oblong pits dug into the surface of the desert sand. The deceased was rolled up in a mat or laid directly on the ground, and the sum total of his or her funerary equipment consisted of a few baked clay vessels and some amulets.

BODY AND SOULS UNITED IN MUMMIFICATION

Developed as early as the Third Dynasty, mummification was another of the material safeguards serving to protect against the dangers of the passage into the hereafter. If the spiritual and physical elements of individuals were to be reunited after death, it was necessary to preserve the integrity of their fleshly container and avoid its decay at any cost. Noting that a body placed directly into the sand experienced a natural dessication that assured it a good state of preservation (Figure 38), the Egyptians developed ever more sophisticated techniques of improving on the spontaneous effects of the desert. In this case as well, mummification, which would become common in the first millennium, was reserved in the age of the pyramids for the royal family and those of highest rank. The earliest attempts consisted in wrap-

FIGURE 38.
Reconstruction of a prehistoric burial, including a body that experienced natural dessication. University of Pennsylvania Museum, Philadelphia, neg. # S4-134562. Photo courtesy of the University of Pennsylvania Museum, Philadelphia.

ping bodies, left as they were, with bandages coated with resin. Around 2600 B.C.E., evisceration of the body began to be practiced; after their removal, the organs were ritually placed in specific vases called canopic jars. The flesh was then dried out by covering it with natron, which had a sodium carbonate base, after which the body was carefully wrapped in bandages. The successive layers of bandages wrapped around the body of Wah, an official personage from around 2000, had a total surface area of nearly 450 square yards. Facial features were sometimes painted on the bands of cloth covering the head, indicating to the archaeologist whether the body is that of a man or a woman.

After mummification, the opening of the mouth ritual was carried out; the ritual consisted of magical formulas and ritual acts supposed to endow the body with the functional capacities of its mouth, eyes, nose, and ears, thus enabling it to perform "normal" activities in the hereafter: speaking, breathing, moving about, and consuming the offerings intended for it. With the material preparation of the body completed, one could proceed to the burial, in which learned ritualists engaged in magicoreligious practices intended to assure its survival.

THE FUNERAL CEREMONY

Most often, it was necessary to cross the Nile to reach the side of the cemeteries, which were watched over by the gods Osiris and Anubis. The deceased was laid out in his or her coffin, which we today call a sarcophagus, and hauled onto a boat for the final journey. Nearby was a statue, which represented the deceased with the features of youth and which would serve as a double in case of physical damage to the bodily shell. Upon arrival on the opposite bank, the catafalque was drawn to the tomb by oxen. Professional mourning women accompanied the cortege, crying out in grief like the goddesses Isis and Nephthys mourning their brother Osiris. The Muu, specialized actor-dancers with braided flowers on their heads, performed propitiatory dances. The priests conducted the ceremony, in which the family and close relatives of the deceased participated. In the "Story of Sinuhe," a fictional text of the Middle Kingdom, the pharaoh urges the hero, who is exiled in Syria, to return to his native country so as to have an Egyptian burial, which alone could assure him eternal salvation. "Think of the day of burial, of the passage to the state of glorification. Darkness will then be assigned to you, and the oils (needed for embalming), and the bandages that are in the hands of Tayt (the goddess of weaving). One will make a funeral procession for you on the day of burial, with a sarcophagus of gold whose head will be of lapis lazuli. . . . Oxen will drag you, singers will precede you, the dance of the Muu will be done for you at the entrance to your tomb. A list of offerings will be recited for you; sacrifices will be carried out before your offering tables; and the columns (of your tomb) will be erected of white stone among the tombs of the royal children. You must not die in a foreign land; the Asiatics will not bury you."

Once a coffin was laid on the floor of the burial chamber, the cortege arranged the funerary equipment around it, hoping to furnish the deceased with ritual objects capable of facilitating his life in the hereafter. A little of everything was to be found around the deceased: wares to hold food, alabaster containers for oils and unguents, headrests, chests containing cloth and clothing, sandals, canopic jars filled with the viscera (in case the deceased came to miss these organs beyond the tomb), a mirror, toilet objects, musical instruments, games, one or two scribal palettes, and sometimes weapons and sticks, and, beginning with the Middle Kingdom, *ushabtis*, little figurines representing the deceased and charged with magically taking the deceased's place in any corvée labor that awaited in the afterlife.

In the Old Kingdom, the decoration of a tomb recalled the major activities of its owner and the most pleasant moments of his life. Beginning with the Middle Kingdom, tombs displaying so sumptuous a carved decoration were less common. But we see the development of a more varied funerary equipment, augmented by painted wooden models, miniature reproductions, after a fashion, of the surroundings of the deceased: what had formerly adorned the walls of the chapels was now represented in three dimensions around the sarcophagus. The tomb of Meketre at Deir el-Bahri (c. 2000 B.C.E.) contained twenty-five of these models, certain of which are veritable scale models of scenes of daily life. Scattered pell-mell were fishing boats with their fishermen and their fish, scribes making a record of numerous cattle, weaving and carpentry workshops, and boats laden with people depicting either the pilgrimage to Abydos or the funeral crossing to the riverbank of the dead. The sarcophagi themselves were decorated with friezes of objects whose very depiction, thanks to the magic that gave life to every representation, was supposed to provide for the needs of the deceased. Additionally, on the insides of the coffins there were written the Coffin Texts, formulas inspired by the Pyramid Texts once reserved for the pharaohs alone. From then on, ordinary mortals would be able to benefit from the posthumous destiny of the kings, conquering the enemies of the celestial voyage in the hereafter through the magic of these ritual words and achieving immortality, like the kings, with the god Re, who still shared authority with Osiris over the kingdom of the dead.

THE CULT OF THE DEAD

Dead and buried, the departed one still had need of specific services and rituals, which we call the funerary cult. This last was carried out in the tomb chapel, which remained accessible to visitors and the offerings they regularly brought. To survive, an Egyptian could not be satisfied with what he or she brought along on the day of burial. The living also had to place oils and fresh food, year after year, festival after festival, on the offering table or the altar of the chapel. To assure that the offering ritual would not be forgotten, it was common to have offering bearers carved on the walls of the chapel, and to inscribe "placards," which were interminable lists naming desired products and their appropriate quantities (Figure 39). An "ap-

FIGURE 39.
Princess Nofret-iabet seated before a table; above and to the right of the table are a "placard" listing types and quantities of offerings. From an Old Kingdom mastaba. Louvre E22745. © Musée du Louvre. Photo courtesy of The Louvre.

peal to the living" inspired the latter to pronounce these names out loud, in the hope that the magic of the word would lend them substance and reality. For the nobles, the service of the funerary cult was assured by priests called "*ka*-servants," with whom one could make a contract before one's death. In return for the cession of certain of his private goods, the governor Dje-faihapy (c. 1950 B.C.E.) required in writing that all the rituals and all the ceremonies that would follow his burial be carried out by his funerary priest, as stipulated, with the desired quantities of offerings.

The posthumous cult of a pharaoh required the service of a temple all his own. Built next to the pyramid of the king, the Fifth Dynasty temple of Neferirkare-Kakai at Abusir has yielded a portion of its administrative papyri, revealing the economic system of its organization. From these archives, we learn that the daily service of this funerary cult carried on at least two hundred years after the death of the king, employing about thirty persons who worked in rotation on the provision and storage of supplies. Besides the priests, the duty rosters name artisans, launderers, cooks, and porters, who were all the beneficiaries of the offerings after the completion of the daily rituals, using them to feed their families.

DEATH IS NOT AN END...

The Egyptians did not rule out the possibility that their dead could intervene in the world of the living. The sudden death of a wife after a domestic quarrel, or of a father who was neglected in the last moments of his life, would inspire remorse in the survivors, who feared that the spirit of the dead would return like a phantom to take vengeance by making their lives impossible. If the departed was simply a loved one missed by those remaining, one had no fear but rather wrote to ask for advice and protection. The "letters to the dead" form a very special category in the pharaonic documentation, for they provide a glimpse into the intimate relationships that Egyptians continued to maintain with their close relatives, even after their death. Quite often, these letters are scrawled in hieratic on baked-clay containers filled with offerings and placed above the grave of the deceased. To drive out the evil fate hovering over her household and making her servants ill, the widow Dedi (c. 2000 B.C.E.) wrote to her late husband, "Sent by Dedi to the priest Inyotef, born of Iunakhte: 'As for this servant Imiu who is ill, can you not fight night and day for her against any man or any woman who wishes her harm? Why do you want to spoil everything? Fight for her again! Now! Then her household will be restored and libations will be made for you. If you do not help us, your house will be destroyed! Don't you know that it is this servant who does everything amongst the people? Fight for [her]! Watch over her! . . . Then your house and your children will be well. Hear me well!'" The earliest letters to the dead appeared in the time of the pyramids, about 2350. They always manifest quite a lively tone, sometimes affectionate, sometimes threatening, expressing sentiments one might think would have been reserved for the living.

In these vehement addresses to the dead, we must see an additional proof of the passion peculiar to the human race and especially present in the hearts of the Egyptians, who poured all their energy into the denial of death and a refusal to see in it an end to the stuff of life.

BIBLIOGRAPHY

In the general bibliography, the reader will find the works to which the author referred on the subjects treated in this book. There follows a list of the anthologies of scholarly translations of Egyptian texts, both secular and religious, which are quoted at length throughout this book. Finally, there is a chapter-by-chapter bibliography in which readers will be able to find what further, detailed information their own curiosity may lead them to seek on specific topics. Most of the works cited below include highly detailed bibliographies of their own, which it seemed unnecessary to repeat here.

GENERAL BIBLIOGRAPHY

Andreu, Guillemette. *Images de la vie quotidienne en Égypte au temps des pharaons*. Paris: Hachette, 1992.

Baines, John, and Jaromír Málek. *Atlas of Ancient Egypt*. New York: Facts on File, 1980.

Cherpion, Nadine. *Mastabas et hypogées d'Ancien Empire: Le problème de la datation*. Brussels: Connaissance de l'Égypte Ancienne, 1989.

Daumas, François. *La civilisation de l'Égypte ancienne*. Paris: Arthaud, 1967.

Donadoni, Sergio, ed. *L'homme égyptien*. Paris: Le Seuil, 1992.

Donadoni Roveri, Anna Maria, ed. *Egyptian Civilization: Egyptian Museum of Turin*. Milan: Electa, 1987–1989.

Eggebrecht, Arne, et al. *L'Égypte ancienne*. Paris: Bordas, 1986.

Erman, Adolf, and Herman Ranke. *La civilisation égyptienne*, trans. Charles Mathien. Paris: Payot, 1963. Originally published as *Ägypten und ägyptisches Leben im Altertum*. Tübinger: Mohr, 1923.

Grimal, Nicolas. *Histoire de l'Égypte ancienne*. Paris: Fayard, 1988. Trans. Ian Shaw under the title *A History of Ancient Egypt* (Oxford: Blackwell, 1992).

Harpur, Yvonne. *Decoration in Egyptian Tombs of the Old Kingdom: Studies on Orientation and Scene Content*. London: Routledge & Kegan Paul, 1987.

Helck, Wolfgang, Eberhard Otto, and Wolfhart Westendorf, eds. *Lexikon der Ägyptologie*. 7 vols. Wiesbaden: Otto Harrassowitz, 1975–1992.

Histoire des religions. Vol. 1, *Religions antiques, religions de salut*. Paris: Encyclopédie de la Pléiade, 1970.

Histoire universelle. Vol. 1, *Des origines à l'Islam*. Paris: Encyclopédie de la Pléiade, 1956.

Leclant, Jean, et al. *Les pharaons: Le temps des pyramides*. Paris: Gallimard, 1978.

Malek, Jaromir. *In the Shadow of the Pyramids: Egypt during the Old Kingdom*. Norman: University of Oklahoma Press, 1986.

Mariette, Auguste. *Les mastabas de l'Ancien Empire*. Published from the author's manuscript by G. Maspero, Paris: 1889. Reprint, Hildesheim: Olms, 1976.

Midant-Reynes, Béatrix. *Préhistoire de l'Égypte: Des premiers hommes aux premiers pharaons*. Paris: Colin, 1992.

Montet, Pierre. *Les scènes de la vie privée dans les tombeaux égyptiens de l'Ancien Empire*. Strasbourg: Librairie Istra, 1925.

Posener, Georges, Serge Sauneron, and Jean Yoyotte. *Dictionnaire de la civilisation égyptienne*. Paris: Hazan, 1959.

Stead, Miriam. *Egyptian Life*. London: British Museum, 1986.

Strouhal, Evžen. *Život Starých Egypťanů*. Prague: Panorama, 1989. Trans. Deryck Viney as Eugen Strouhal, *Life of the Ancient Egyptians* (Norman: University of Oklahoma Press, 1992).

Trigger, B. G., B. J. Kemp, D. O'Connor, and A. B. Lloyd. *Ancient Egypt: A Social History*. Cambridge: Cambridge University Press, 1983.

Valbelle, Dominique. *L'égyptologie*. Paris: Presses Universitaires de France, 1991.

———. *La vie dans l'Égypte ancienne,* Paris: Presses Universitaires de France, 1988.

Vandier, Jacques. *Manuel d'archéologie égyptienne*. 6 vols. Paris: Picard, 1952–1969.

Vercoutter, Jean. *L'Égypte et la vallée du Nil*. Vol. 1, *Des origines à la fin de l'Ancien Empire*. Paris: Presses Universitaires de France, 1992.

Vernus, Pascal, and Jean Yoyotte. *Les pharaons*. Paris: MA Éditions, 1988.

Wildung, Dietrich. *L'âge d'or de l'Égypte: Le Moyen Empire*. Trans. Suzanne Bickel, Sandra Poggia-Garnori, and Jean-Luc Chappaz. Paris: Presses Universitaires de France, 1984. Originally published as *Sesostris und Amenemhet: Ägypten im Mittleren Reich* (Munich: Hirmer, 1984).

ANTHOLOGIES OF TRANSLATIONS OF TEXTS
FROM THE AGE OF THE PYRAMIDS

Breasted, James Henry. *Ancient Records of Egypt*. Vol. 1, *The First to the Seventeenth Dynasties*. Reprint, New York: Russell & Russell, 1962.

Lalouette, Claire. *Textes sacrés et textes profanes de l'ancienne Égypte*. Vol. 1, *Des pharaons et des hommes*. Vol. 2, *Mythes, contes, et poésie*. Paris: Gallimard, 1984 and 1987.

Lefebvre, Gustave. *Romans et contes égyptiens de l'époque pharaonique*. Paris: Maisonneuve, 1949.

Lichtheim, Miriam. *Ancient Egyptian Autobiographies Chiefly of the Middle Kingdom: A Study and an Anthology*. Göttingen and Freiburg: Vandenhoeck & Ruprecht and Universitätsverlag, 1988.

———. *Ancient Egyptian Literature: A Book of Readings*. Vol. 1, *The Old and Middle Kingdoms*. Berkeley: University of California Press, 1975.

Parkinson, Richard B. *Voices from Ancient Egypt: An Anthology of Middle Kingdom Writings.* London: British Museum, 1991.

Posener, Georges. "Le conte de Neferkaré et du général Siséné." *Revue d'Égyptologie* 11 (1957): 119–37.

———. *L'enseignement loyaliste: Sagesse égyptienne du Moyen Empire.* Geneva: Droz, 1976.

Rocatti, Alessandro. *La littérature historique sous l'Ancien Empire égyptien.* Paris: Cerf, 1982.

Simpson, William Kelly, ed. *The Literature of the Ancient Egyptians.* New Haven: Yale University Press, 1973.

Wente, Edward F. *Letters from Ancient Egypt.* Atlanta: Scholars Press, 1990.

THE AGE OF THE PYRAMIDS

Butzer, Karl W. *Early Hydraulic Civilization in Egypt: A Study in Cultural Ecology.* Chicago: University of Chicago Press, 1976.

L'Égypte avant les pyramides, 4e millénaire. Paris: Grand Palais, 1973.

L'Égypte des millénaires obscurs. Marseille: Hatier et Musées de Marseille, 1990.

Emery, Walter B. *Archaic Egypt.* Baltimore: Penguin Books, 1961.

Mémoires d'Égypte. Paris: Bibliothèque Nationale, 1990.

Naissance de l'écriture: Cunéiformes et hiéroglyphes. Paris: Éditions de la Réunion des Musées Nationaux, 1982.

Spencer, A. J. *Early Egypt: The Rise of Civilisation in the Nile Valley.* London: British Museum, 1993.

Stadelmann, Rainer. "Beiträge zur Geschichte des Alten Reich: Die Länge der Regierung des Snofru." *Mitteilungen des Deutschen Archäologischen Instituts Abteilung Kairo* 43 (1987): 229–40.

Vernus, Pascal. "La naissance de l'écriture dans l'Égypte ancienne." *Archéo-Nil* 3 (1993): 75–108.

PHARAOH'S SUBJECTS

Assmann, Jan. *Maât: L'Égypte pharaonique et l'idée de justice sociale.* Paris: Julliard, 1989.

Baer, Klaus. *Rank and Title in the Old Kingdom.* Chicago: University of Chicago Press, 1960.

Berlev, Oleg. *Social Relations in Egypt in the Middle Kingdom* (in Russian). Moscow: Nauka, 1978.

———. *The Working Class in Egypt in the Middle Kingdom* (in Russian). Moscow: Nauka, 1972.

Bonhême, Marie-Ange, and Annie Forgeau. *Pharaon: Les secrets d'un pouvoir.* Paris: Colin, 1988.

Hayes, William C. *A Papyrus of the Late Middle Kingdom.* 2d ed. New York: Brooklyn Museum, 1972.

Helck, Wolfgang, *Untersuchungen zu den Beamtentiteln des ägyptischen Alten Reiches*. Hamburg: J. J. Augustin, 1954.

———. *Zur Verwaltung des Mittleren und Neuen Reichs*. Leiden: Brill, 1958.

Husson, Geneviève, and Dominique Valbelle. *L'état et les institutions en Égypte des premiers pharaons aux empereurs romains*. Paris: Colin, 1992.

Kanawati, Naguib. *The Egyptian Administration in the Old Kingdom: Evidence on Its Economic Decline*. Warminster, England: Aris & Phillips, 1977.

———. *Governmental Reforms in Old Kingdom Egypt*. Warminster, England: Aris & Phillips, 1980.

Lichtheim, Miriam. *Maat in Egyptian Autobiographies and Related Studies*. Göttingen and Freiburg: Vandenhoeck & Ruprecht and Universitätsverlag, 1992.

Martin-Pardey, Eva. *Untersuchungen zur ägyptischen Provinzialverwaltung bis zum Ende des Alten Reiches*. Hildesheim: Gerstenberg, 1976.

Posener, Georges. "Les Asiatiques en Égypte sous les XIIe et XIIIe dynasties." *Syria* 34 (1957): 145–63.

———. *De la divinité du pharaon*. Paris: Imprimerie Nationale, 1960.

———. *L'enseignement loyaliste: Sagesse égyptienne du Moyen Empire*. Geneva: Droz, 1976.

———. *Littérature et politique dans l'Égypte de la XIIe dynastie*. Paris: Librairie Champion, 1969.

Quirke, Stephen. *The Administration of Egypt in the Late Middle Kingdom: The Hieratic Documents*. New Malden, England: SIA Publications, 1990.

Redford, Donald B. "Egypt and Western Asia in the Old Kingdom." *Journal of the American Research Center in Egypt* 23 (1986): 125–44.

Simpson, William Kelly. *The Terrace of the Great God at Abydos: The Offering Chapels of Dynasties 12 and 13*. New Haven and Philadelphia: Peabody Museum and University Museum of Archaeology and Anthropology, 1974.

Strudwick, Nigel. *The Administration of Egypt in the Old Kingdom: The Highest Titles and Their Holders*. London: Kegan Paul International, 1985.

Valbelle, Dominique. *Les Neuf Arcs: L'Égyptien et les étrangers de la préhistoire à la conquête d'Alexandre*. Paris: Colin, 1990.

Van den Boorn, G. P. F. *The Duties of the Vizier: Civil Administration in the Early New Kingdom*. London: Kegan Paul International, 1988.

PUBLIC WORKS

Andreu, Guillemette. "Les Égyptiens au Sinaï." *Le Monde de la Bible* 10 (1979): 26–28.

Arnold, Dieter. *Building in Egypt*. New York: Oxford University Press, 1991.

Berlev, Oleg. Review of Ashraf Sadek, *The Amethyst Mining Inscriptions of Wadi el-Hudi*. *Bibliotheca Orientalis* 40 (1983): 355–57.

Castel, Georges, Jean-François Gout, and Georges Soukiassian. "Découverte de mines pharaoniques au bord de la mer Rouge." *Archéologia* 192/193 (August 1984): 44–57.

Castel, Georges, and Georges Soukiassian. "Dépôt de stèles dans le sanctuaire du Nouvel Empire au Gebel Zeit." *Bulletin de l'Institut Français d'Archéologie Orientale du Caire* 85 (1985): 285–93.

Cénival, Jean-Louis de, and Henri Stierlin. *Égypte: Architecture universelle.* Freiburg: Office du Livre, 1964.

Golvin, Jean-Claude and Jean-Claude Goyon. *Les bâtisseurs de Karnak.* Paris: CNRS, 1987.

Goyon, Georges. "Les navires de transport de la chaussée monumentale d'Ounas." *Bulletin de l'Institut Français d'Archéologie Orientale du Caire* 69 (1971) 11–42.

Lauer, Jean-Philippe. *Le Mystère des pyramides.* Paris: Presses de la Cité, 1988.

———. *Les Pyramides de Saqqarah.* 6th ed. Cairo: Institut Français d'Archéologie Orientale du Caire, 1991.

———. *Saqqarah: La nécropole royale de Memphis, quarante siècles d'histoire.* Paris: Tallandier, 1976. Published in English as *Saqqara, the Royal Cemetery of Memphis: Excavations and Discoveries since 1850* (New York: Scribner's, 1976).

Posener, Georges. "L'anachorésis dans L'Égypte ancienne." In *Le monde grec: Hommages à Claire Préaux.* Brussels: Université Libre de Bruxelles, 1975.

Seyfried, Karl-Joachim. *Beiträge zu den Expeditionen des Mittleren Reiches in die Ost-Wüste.* Hildesheim: Gerstenberg, 1981.

Stadelmann, Rainer. *Die ägyptischen Pyramiden.* Mainz am Rhein: Philipp von Zabern, 1985.

———. "La ville de pyramide à l'Ancien Empire." *Revue d'Égyptologie* 33 (1981): 67–77.

Valbelle, Dominique. "Le Sinaï des pharaons." *Le Monde de la Bible* 82 (May/June 1993): 15–18.

Watson, Philip J. *Egyptian Pyramids and Mastaba Tombs.* Aylesbury, England: Shire, 1987.

Yoyotte, Jean. "Les sementiou et l'exploitation des régions minières à l'Ancien Empire. *Bulletin de la Société Française d'Égyptologie* 73 (June 1975): 44–55.

SCRIBES AND SCHOLARS

Brunner, Hellmut. "L'éducation en ancienne Égypte." In *Histoire mondiale de l'éducation,* vol. 1. Paris: Presses Universitaires de France, 1981.

———. *Die Lehre des Cheti Sohnes des Duauf.* Glückstadt: J. J. Augustin, 1944. See also the extensive review, with a translation of the Egyptian text into French, by Baudouin Van de Walle, *Chronique d'Égypte* 48 (July 1949): 244–56.

Černý, Jaroslav. "Language and Writing." In *The Legacy of Egypt,* ed. J. R. Harris Oxford: Oxford University Press, 1971.

————. *Paper and Books in Ancient Egypt*. Chicago: Ares, 1952.

Christie, Agatha. *Death Comes as the End*. New York: Dodd, Mead, 1944.

Couchoud, Sylvia. *Mathématiques égyptiennes*. Paris: Le Léopard d'Or, 1993.

Curto, Silvio. *Medicina e medici nell'Antico Egitto*. Turin: Museo Egizio, 1970.

Fischer, Henry George. *L'écriture et l'art de l'Égypte ancienne*. Paris: Presses Universitaires de France, 1986.

Ghaliounghi, Paul. *The Physicians of Pharaonic Egypt*. Cairo: Al-Ahram Center for Scientific Translations, 1983.

Gillins, Richard J. *Mathematics in the Time of the Pharaohs*. Cambridge, Mass.: MIT Press, 1972.

Harris, J. R. "Medicine." In *The Legacy of Egypt*, ed. J. R. Harris Oxford: Oxford University Press, 1971.

James, T. G. H. *The Hekanakhte Papers and Other Early Middle Kingdom Documents*. New York: Metropolitan Museum of Art, 1962.

Naissance de l'écriture: Cunéiformes et hiéroglyphes. Paris: Éditions de la Réunion des Musées Nationaux, 1982.

Parker, Richard A. "The Calendars and Chronology." In *The Legacy of Egypt*, ed. J. R. Harris. Oxford: Oxford University Press, 1971.

————. *The Calendars of Ancient Egypt*. Chicago: University of Chicago Press, 1950.

Parkinson, Richard B. "Teachings, Discourses, and Tales from the Middle Kingdom." In *Middle Kingdom Studies,* ed. Stephen Quirke. New Malden, England: SIA Publications, 1991.

Posener, Georges. "Les richesses inconnues de la littérature égyptienne." *Revue d'Égyptologie* 6 (1951): 27–48 and 9 (1952): 117–20.

Toomer, G. J. "Mathematics and Astronomy." In *The Legacy of Egypt*, ed. J. R. Harris. Oxford: Oxford University Press, 1971.

Vernus, Pascal. "Les espaces de l'écrit dans l'Égypte pharaonique." *Bulletin de la Société Française d'Égyptologie* 119 (1990): 35–56.

Wente, Edward F. *Letters from Ancient Egypt*. Atlanta: Scholars Press, 1990.

ARTS, CRAFTS, AND TRADES

Bonhême, Marie-Ange. *L'art égyptien*. Paris: Presses Universitaires de France, 1992.

Corteggiani, Jean-Pierre. *L'Égypte des pharaons au Musée du Caire*. Paris: Hachette, 1987.

Davis, Whitney M. "Artists and Patrons in Predynastic and Early Dynastic Egypt." *Studien zur altägyptischen Kultur* 10 (1983): 119–39.

Delange, Elisabeth. *Catalogue des statues égyptiennes du Moyen Empire, Musée du Louvre*. Paris: Éditions de la Réunion des Musées Nationaux, 1987.

Fischer, Henry George. *Egyptian Women of the Old Kingdom and of the Heracleopolitan Period*. New York: Metropolitan Museum of Art, 1989.

————. "Les meubles égyptiens." In *L'écriture et l'art de l'Égypte ancienne*. Paris: Presses Universitaires de France, 1986.

Hall, Rosalind. *Egyptian Textiles*. Aylesbury, England: Shire, 1986.

Hope, Colin. *Egyptian Pottery*. Aylesbury, England: Shire, 1987.

James, T. G. H., and W. V. Davies. *Egyptian Painting*. London: British Museum, 1985.

————. *Egyptian Sculpture*. London: British Museum, 1983.

Killen, Geoffrey P. *Ancient Egyptian Furniture*. Vol. 1. Warminster, England: Aris & Phillips, 1980.

Lalouette, Claire. *L'art de la vie dans l'Égypte pharaonique*. Paris: Fayard, 1992.

Lange, Kurt, Max Hirmer, Eberhard Otto, and Christiane Desroches-Noblecourt. *L'Égypte*. Paris: Flammarion, 1968.

Lhôte, André. *Les chefs-d'oeuvre de la peinture égyptienne*. Paris: Hachette, 1954.

Robins, Gay. *Egyptian Painting and Relief*. Aylesbury, England: Shire, 1986.

Saleh, Mohamed, and Hourig Sourouzian. *Catalogue officiel du Musée du Caire*. Mainz: Zabern, 1987.

Schäfer, Heinrich. *Von ägyptischer Kunst, besonders der Zeichenkunst: Eine Einführung in die Betrachtung ägyptischer Kunstwerke*. Leipzig: J. C. Hinrichs'sche Buchhandlung, 1919. Trans. John Baines under the title *Principles of Egyptian Art* (Oxford: Clarendon, 1974).

Scheel, Bernd. *Egyptian Metalworking and Tools*. Aylesbury, England: Shire, 1989.

Smith, William Stevenson. *The Art and Architecture of Ancient Egypt*. 2d ed. New York: Penguin, 1981.

————. *A History of Egyptian Sculpture and Painting in the Old Kingdom*. 2d ed. Boston: Museum of Fine Arts, 1946.

Soukiassian, Georges, Michel Wuttmann, Laure Pantalacci, Pascale Ballet, and Michel Picon. *Balat III: Les ateliers de potiers d'Ayn-Asil*. Cairo: Institut Français d'Archéologie Orientale du Caire, 1990.

Vandersleyen, Claude. *Das alte Ägypten*. Berlin: Propyläen, 1975.

————. "L'art égyptien." In *Égypte*. Paris: Bordas, 1984.

Wilson, John A. "The Artist of the Egyptian Old Kingdom." *Journal of Near Eastern Studies* 6 (1947): 231–49.

Yoyotte, Jean. *Trésors des Pharaons*. Geneva: Skira, 1968.

Ziegler, Christiane. "L'Égypte." In *Histoire de l'art*. Vol. 1, *Naissance de l'art: De la préhistoire à l'art romain,* ed. Albert Châtelet and Bernard Philippe Groslier Paris: Librairie Larousse Références, 1988.

————. *Le Louvre: Les antiquités égyptiennes*. Paris: Éditions de la Réunion des Musées Nationaux, 1990.

————. *Le mastaba d'Akhethetep, une chapelle funéraire de l'Ancien Empire*. Paris: Éditions de la Réunion des Musées Nationaux, 1993.

FAMILY LIFE

Brunner, Hellmut. "L'éducation en ancienne Égypte." In *Histoire mondiale de l'éducation,* vol. 1. Paris: Presses Universitaires de France, 1981.

David, Rosalind. *The Pyramid Builders of Ancient Egypt: A Modern Investigation of Pharaoh's Workforce.* London: Routledge & Kegan Paul, 1986.

Forgeau, Annie. "La mémoire du nom et l'ordre pharaonique." In *Histoire de la famille.* Paris: Colin, 1986.

Giddy, Lisa L. *Egyptian Oases.* Warminster, England: Aris & Phillips, 1987.

Janssen, Rosalind, and Jac. J. Janssen. *Growing Up in Ancient Egypt.* London: Rubicon, 1990.

Jouer dans l'antiquité. Marseille: Éditions de la Réunion des Musées Nationaux, 1991.

Laskowska-Kusztal, Ewa. "Un atelier de perruquier à Deir el-Bahari." *Études et Travaux* 10 (1978): 82–120.

Robins, Gay. *Women in Ancient Egypt.* London: British Museum, 1993.

Simpson, William Kelly. "Polygamy in Egypt in the Middle Kingdom?" *Journal of Egyptian Archaeology* 60 (1974): 100–105.

Soukiassian, Georges, Michel Wuttmann, and Daniel Schaad. "La Ville d'Ayn-Asil à Dakhla: État des recherches." *Bulletin de l'Institut Français d'Archéologie Orientale du Caire* 90 (1990): 347–58.

Uphill, Eric. *Egyptian Towns and Cities.* Aylesbury, England: Shire, 1988.

Valbelle, Dominique. "L'Égypte pharaonique." In Dominique Valbelle, Jean-Louis Huot, and Jean-Paul Thalmann, *Naissance des cités.* Paris: Nathan, 1990.

Vernus, Pascal. *Le surnom au Moyen Empire.* Rome: Pontifical Biblical Institute, 1986.

Yoyotte, Jean. "Les jeux des enfants et des adolescents en Égypte." *Les Dossiers d'Archéologie* 168 (February 1992): 2–7.

A BUSY DAY

Andrews, Carol. *Ancient Egyptian Jewellery.* London: British Museum, 1990.

Bellessort, Marie-Noël. "Le jeu de serpent." *Les Dossiers d'Archéologie* 168 (February 1992): 8–9.

Brunner-Traut, Emma. *Der Tanz im alten Ägypten.* Glückstadt: J. J. Augustin, 1958.

Darby, William J., Paul Ghaliounghi, and Louis Grivetti. *Food: The Gift of Osiris.* 2 vols. New York: Academic Press, 1977.

Decker, Wolfgang. *Sports and Games of Ancient Egypt.* Cairo: American University of Cairo, 1993.

La femme au temps des pharaons. Brussels: L. Pernoud, 1985.

Hall, Rosalind. *Egyptian Textiles.* Aylesbury, England: Shire, 1986.

Janssen, Rosalind, and Jac. J. Janssen. *Egyptian Household Animals.* Aylesbury, England: Shire, 1989.

———. *Growing Up in Ancient Egypt*. London: Rubicon, 1990.

Vandier d'Abbadie, Jeanne. *Catalogue des objets de toilette égyptiens*. Paris: Musée du Louvre, 1972.

Wilson, Hilary. *Egyptian Food and Drink*. Aylesbury, England: Shire, 1988.

Ziegler, Christiane. *Les instruments de musique égyptiens au Musée du Louvre*. Paris: Éditions de la Réunion des Musées Nationaux, 1979.

LIFE IN THE COUNTRY

Caminos, Ricardo A. "Le paysan." In *L'homme égyptien,* ed. Sergio Donadoni Paris: Seuil, 1992.

Kueny, Gabrielle. "Scènes apicoles dans l'Ancienne Égypte." *Journal of Near Eastern Studies* 9 (1950): 84–93.

Lerstrup, Annette. "The Making of Wine in Egypt." *Göttinger Miszellen* 129 (1992): 61–82.

Mathieu, Bernard. "Études de métrique égyptien. II, Contraintes métriques et production textuelle dans l'*Hymne à la crue du Nil*." *Revue d'Égyptologie* 41 (1990): 127–41.

Vandier, Jacques. *La famine dans l'Égypte ancienne*. Cairo: Institut Français d'Archéologie Orientale du Caire, 1936.

Ziegler, Christiane. *Le mastaba d'Akhethetep, une chapelle funéraire de l'Ancien Empire*. Paris: Éditions de la Réunion des Musées Nationaux, 1993.

FISHING AND HUNTING

Altenmüller, Hartwig. *Jagd im alten Ägypten*. Hamburg: Parey, 1967.

Brewers, Douglas, and René Friedman. *Fish and Fishing in Ancient Egypt*. Warminster, England: Aris & Phillips, 1989.

Daumas, François. "Quelques remarques sur les représentations de pêche à la ligne sous l'Ancien Empire." *Bulletin de l'Institut Français d'Archéologie Orientale* 62 (1964): 67–85.

Houlihan, Patrick F. *The Birds of Ancient Egypt*. Vol. 1, *The Natural History of Egypt*. Warminster, England: Aris & Phillips, 1986.

Vandier, Jacques. "Quelques remarques sur la préparation de la boutargue." *Kêmi* 17 (1964): 26–34.

Ziegler, Christiane. *Le mastaba d'Akethetep, une chapelle funéraire de l'Ancien Empire*. Paris: Éditions de la Réunion des Musées Nationaux, 1993.

A PEOPLE OF BELIEVERS

Assmann, Jan. *Maât: L'Égypte pharaonique et l'idée de justice sociale*. Paris: Julliard, 1989.

Breasted, James Henry. *Egyptian Servant Statues*. New York: Pantheon, 1948.

Derchain, Philippe. Numerous articles on ancient Egypt in *Dictionnaire des mythologies,* ed. Yves de Bonnefoy. Paris: Flammarion, 1981. Published in English as *Mythologies* (Chicago: University of Chicago Press, 1991).

Donadoni, Sergio. "Le mort." In *L'homme égyptien,* ed. Sergio Donadoni. Paris: Seuil, 1992.

Dunand, Françoise, and Roger Lichtenberg. *Les momies: Un voyage dans l'éternité.* Paris: Découvertes Gallimard, 1991.

Dunand, Françoise, and Christiane Zivie-Coche. *Dieux et hommes en Égypte.* Paris: Colin, 1991.

Franco, Isabelle. *Rites et croyances d'éternité.* Paris: Pygmalion, 1993.

Gardiner, Alan H., and Kurt Sethe. *Egyptian Letters to the Dead: Mainly from the Old and Middle Kingdoms.* London: Oxford University Press, 1928.

Hornung, Erik. *Der Eine und die Vielen: Ägyptische Gottesvorstellungen.* Darmstadt: Wissenschaftliche Buchgesellschaft, 1973. Trans. John Baines under the title of *Conceptions of God in Ancient Egypt: The One and the Many,* Ithaca: Cornell University Press, 1996.

Lichtheim, Miriam. *Ancient Egyptian Autobiographies Chiefly of the Middle Kingdom: A Study and an Anthology.* Göttingen and Freiburg: Vandenhoeck & Ruprecht and Universitätsverlag, 1988.

Meeks, Dimitri, and Christine Favard-Meeks. *La vie quotidienne des dieux égyptiens.* Paris: Hachette, 1993. Trans. G. M. Goshgarian under the title *Daily Life of the Egyptian Gods.* Ithaca: Cornell University Press, 1996.

Posener-Kriéger, Paule. *Les archives du temple funéraire de Néferirkarê-Kakaï: Traduction et commentaire.* 2 vols. Cairo: Institut Français d'Archéologie Orientale du Caire, 1976.

Sauneron, Serge, and Jean Yoyotte. *La naissance du monde.* Paris: Seuil, 1959.

Simpson, William Kelly. *The Terrace of the Great God at Abydos: The Offering Chapels of Dynasties 12 and 13.* New Haven and Philadelphia: Peabody Museum and University Museum of Archaeology and Anthropology, 1974.

Traunecker, Claude. *Les dieux de l'Égypte.* Paris: Presses Universitaires de France, 1991.

Wild, Henri. *Les danses sacrés.* Paris: Seuil, 1963.

Yoyotte, Jean. *Le jugement des morts.* Paris: Seuil, 1961.

———. *Les pélerinages.* Paris: Seuil, 1960.

———. "La pensée préphilosophique en Égypte." In *Histoire de la philosophie,* vol. 1. Paris: Encyclopédie de la Pléiade, 1969.

GENERAL INDEX

Page references in italics denote illustrations. References in bold italics indicate text and an illustration on the same page.

Abu Ghurab, 8

Abu Rawash, 12, 39

Abusir, 8, 12, 90, 122, 149;
slaughterhouse annex at, 96

Abydos, 7, 9, 12, 99, 142–43

Administrative structures, 9, 10,
17–20

Adoption, 79

Adoration of the Two Lands (ship), 67

Africa, 2, 12, 21, 74, 103; products
from, 8, 23, 66. *See also* Nubia

Agriculture, 1–2; apiculture, 122;
gardens, *110*, 115–16; and
irrigation, 9, 108–10; and livestock,
112, 117–22; and Nile inundation,
105–8, 116–17; orchards, 116;
plowing and sowing, 111–12;
reaping and harvesting, 112–14,
114; vineyards, 116–17

Ain-Asil, 85

Akhet, 3, 107–8

Alexander the Great, 4

el-Amarna, 29

Amenemhet, 110

Amenemhet I, 14, 15–16, 50

Amenemhet III, 11

Amenemmes. *See* Amenemhet

Amenhotep. *See* Amenophis

Amenhotpe. *See* Amenophis

Amenophis, 21

Amenophis IV (Akhenaten), 138

Ameny, 32, 106

Amulets, 93–94

Amun, 10, 137

Anachoresis, 28

Andalusia, 101

Animal cults, 5, 7, 137–38

Animals, domestic, 87, 96, 112, 117–
22; as pets, 83, 98–99. *See also*
Hunting

Ankhmahor, 78, 83

Antef. *See* Inyotef

Anubis, 7, 147

Any, 76

Apiculture, 122

Archaeology, 11–12; at Ain-Asil, 85;
at Balat, 12, 69, 82, 107; at Deir
el-Bahri, 91; at Gebel Zeit, 33–34;
at el-Lahun, 12, 82, 85–87;
Lauer's work in, 40, 41, 42; in
Nubia, 12, 24–25; at workers'
village in Giza, 42

Army, 21–24

Art: anonymity of, 61; conventions of,
59–60; painting, 47, 62–63, 107;
purpose of, 58–59; relief sculpture,
5, 61–62, 107; training in, 60–61.
See also Statues

Artist/artisans, 58; anonymity of, 61;
class status of, 68, 71; gender of,
71–73; metalworkers, 68–69;
training of, 60–61; and
woodworkers' guild, 66. *See also*
specific arts, crafts, and trades

Asia, 21–22, 28, 50, 76, 147; trade
with, 8, 25–26. *See also* Bedouins

Assiut. *See* Asyut

Assuan. *See* Aswan

Astronomy, 55–56

Aswan, 2, 9, 10, 12; Harkhuf's tomb
at, 23; High Dam at, 11, 24, 84, 105;
mining and quarrying at, 36, 37

Asyut, 109
Atum, 141

Bahr Yusuf, 110
Balat, 9, 12, 82, 107; cemetery at, 85, 145; pottery workshops at, 69
Basketry, 73
Bas-reliefs, 62, 107
Bedouins, 7, 10, 21, 22–23, 28; trade with, 25–26
Beekeeping, 122
Beer, 95
Beni Hasan, 12, 95, 124, 126; Ameny's tomb at, 106; Khety's tomb at, 102–3, *103*, *104*, *115*, *116*; Khnumhotpe's tomb at, 25–26, 72
Bes, 78
Big Dipper, 55
Birds: hunting, 124–26; raising, 121–22
Blacksmithing, 68
Block statues, 64, *64–65*
Board games, 98, *99–100*
Boats, 36–37, *38*, 67–68; of papyrus, 107–8, *131*, 132
Boomerangs, *124*, 124–25
Bread, **95**
Buhen, 24
Burial. *See* Funerary beliefs; Mastabas; Pyramids; Tombs
Butchering, 96, *120*, 120–21
Byblos, 11, 23

Cairo Museum, 59, 65
Calcite, 29–30
Calendar, 3, 55–56
Canals. *See* Irrigation
Carpentry, 66–68
Cats, domestication of, 83, 87
Cattle, 117–21, *119*, *120*, 131
Cattle counts, 119–20

Cemeteries. *See* Mastabas; Pyramids; Tombs
Ceramic workshops. *See* Pottery
Champollion, Jean-François, 4
Chaos (Nun), 139, 140
Cheops. *See* Khufu
Childbirth, 78–80
Children, 77–80, 81; fishing by, 130–31; games and toys of, 82–83; hair of, 82; and hunting, 126; naming of, 79, 137; nudity of, 80, 82; and transition to adulthood, 83–84
Christie, Agatha, 54
Circumcision, 83
Civil service, 20, 45, 66
Clappers, 101–2
Class status: of artist/artisans, 68, 71; and burial, 73, 143, 145; and corvée labor, 28; and the military, 24; of scribes, 10, 19–20, 45–46, 108
Climate, 3, 9
Clothing, 80, 82, 89–90, *90*; of pharaohs, 14
Cobbling, 71
Colonialism, 8, 9, 11, 12, 23; and life of colonists, 24–25
Colors, significance of, 62
Concubines, 76, 79
Construction: of houses, 85–86; of pyramids, 27–28, 40–42
Coptic language, 44
Coptus. *See* Koptos
Correspondence, 53–57, 150
Corvée labor, 27–28, 42
Cosmetics, 92
Crafts and trades: basketry, 73; carpentry, 66–68; leatherwork, 71; metalwork, 68–69, *69*; pottery, 5, 69–71, *70*, 97; spinning and weaving, 71–72, 89; stonecutting, 5, 6, 41–42, 65–66, 97–98
Creation myths, 138–39

Crocodiles, 123, 129
Crowns, 14

Dahshur, 8, 12, 39, 42, 93
Daily life: clothing for, 80, 82, 89–90;
    of families, 86–87; food, 94–98,
    126–27; grooming, 88–92; jewelry
    for, 92–94; research sources on,
    11–12. *See also* Recreation
el-Dakhla Oasis, 9, 12, 107, 116, 145;
    Ain Asil site in, 85; pottery
    workshops in, 69
Dance, 102, *103*, 103–4
Dariut, 36
Dashur. *See* Dahshur
Dead, cult of, 43, 148–50
Death: art as overcoming, 59; denial
    of, 150; and enjoyment of life, 52,
    100–101; fear of, 144. *See also*
    Funerary beliefs; Mastabas;
    Pyramids; Tombs
Decimal system, 54
Dedi, 150
Dedusobk, 20
Deir el-Bahari. *See* Deir el-Bahri
Deir el-Bahri, 91, 148
Deir el-Bersha, 12, 30, *31*, 134–35
Deir el-Gabrawi, 9, 12
Delta, 2, 10, 12, 87, 123; pastures in,
    118; vineyards in, 116
Dendara, 12, 138
Dentistry, 57
Desert, hunting in, 132–36
Determinatives, 4
Dishasha, 22
Divorce, 77
Djau, 45
Djedefre. *See* Radjedef
Djedkare Izezi, 8, 46, 52, 74
Djefaihapy, 149
Djehuti. *See* Thoth
Djehutihotpe, 30–31, *31*

Djehutyhotep. *See* Djehutihotpe
Djoser, 7, *39*, 52, 61
Dogs, 83, 98–99, 134
Dog Star, 3, 55
Dongola, 103
Drums, 102
Dryness season (*shemu*), 3, 112–14

Edfu, 12, 18
Education, 46–47, 53, 84
Egyptian language, 4–5, 49;
    unification of, 44–45
Egyptology, 4–5, 11–12, 40, 137–38
Eighth Dynasty, 10
Elephantine, 33, 37
Eleventh Dynasty, 10, 52, 80
Emergence season (*peret*), 3, 111–12
Ennead, 140
Epagomenal days, 55
Ethiopia, 2

Faiyum, 2, 10, 11, 85, 110
Families: and childbirth, 78–80; daily
    life of, 86–87; housing of, 85–86;
    and marriage and divorce, 74–77;
    and parental love, 77–78. *See also*
    Children
Famines, 106–7
Festivals: inundation, 106; Osirian,
    142–43; *sed*, 7, 15
Fifth Dynasty, 46, 74, 78–79, 97, 119;
    architects during, 40; religion
    during, 8, 138, 149–50; warfare
    during, 22
Fighting, recreational, 102–3, *104*
Figurines. *See* Statues
First Dynasty, 5, 48, 98
First Intermediate Period, 9–10, 19,
    23, 45, 142; pessimistic literature of,
    51, 52. *See also specific dynasties*
Fish and fishing, 2, 5, 97, 126–29,
    127; with harpoons, 130–31

Livestock farming, 112, 117–22
Louvre, 15, 59, 65, 100
Lower Nubia, 23, 24–25
Luxor, 10, 12. *See also* Thebes

Maat, 20, 21, 46, 54, 122; and divine
  punishment, 144; pharaoh's role in
  maintaining, 14, 139
Magic, 57, 129–30
Maidum, 8, 12, 40, 42
Manetho, 7, 8–9
Mariette, Auguste Édouard, 59
Marriage, 74–77
Mars, 55
Marshes, 118, 123–24, 131–32;
  fishing in, 126–29, 130–31;
  hunting in, 124–25, 129–30
el-Masara, 36
Maspero, Gaston-Camille-Charles,
  122
Mastabas, 5, 8, 17–18, 61, 83, 145;
  agricultural scenes on, 110, 111,
  114, 116, 118, 122; fight scenes on,
  102; hunting scenes on, 130, 135;
  marsh scenes on, 123–24, 127–28,
  130. *See also* Funerary beliefs
Mathematics, 54–55
Meals. *See* Food
Measurement, units of, 54–56, 66
Meat, 96–97
Medicine, 56–57
Mediterranean Sea, 2, 21, 25, 126
Mehen, 100
Meir, 82
Meketre, 72, 148
Memphis, 7, 17, 85, 140. *See also*
  Saqqara
Men: clothing of, 89; hair of, 90, 91;
  marriage of, 74–77; recreational
  fighting by, 102–3
Menkauhor, 78
Menkaure, 8

Mentuhotep. *See* Mentuhotpe
Mentuhotpe II, 10
Mentuhotpe Sankhkare, 53
Mercury, 55
Merenre, 18–19
"Merenre Appears in Perfection"
  (name of pyramid), 37
Mereruka, 101, 110
Merykare, 15, 16, 25
Meskhenet, 79
Metalwork, 68–69, 69
Metjen, 115
Middle class, 108; administrative
  positions of, 10, 19–20, 45–46;
  in the army, 24; corvée labor
  exemptions for, 28
Middle Kingdom, 10–11, 33, 85, 107,
  111; administrative reforms of, 10,
  19–20, 45; art of, 61, 64–65; cattle
  counts during, 120; children during,
  80, 82; crafts during, 71, 72; daily
  life during, 93, 95, 100, 102; foreign
  policy during, 11, 23–26; granaries
  during, 114; hunting during, 125,
  126; irrigation during, 109–10;
  literature of, 49–52, 53; peasants'
  status during, 108; pyramids of, 10,
  28, 42, 82; religion during, 138,
  140, 141, 142, 147–48; use of
  honey during, 122
Min, 32–33, 140
Mines and quarries, 29–32; Gebel
  Zeit, 33–34, 34, 35; on the Nile,
  36–37; in Sinai, 11, 29, 33, 34,
  36; Wadi el-Hudi, 33; Wadi
  Hammamat, 11, 30, 32–33
Mirrors, 94, 102
"Mistress of Galena" (Hathor), 34
"Mistress of Sycamore" (Hathor), 116
"Mistress of Turquoise" (Hathor), 36
"Mixed" marriages, 76–77
Moab, 25

el-Moalla, 12
Moeris, Lake, 110
Montu, 10
Mummification, 145–47
Music, 100–102, 103–4
Mut, 79
Muu, 147
Mycerinus. *See* Menkaure

Naga ed-Deir. *See* Nag el-Deir
Nag el-Deir, 12, 57
Neankhkhnum, 78–79, 110
Nebka, 76
Neferefre. *See* Raneferef
Neferirkare-Kakai, 149
Neferkare, 51
Nefermaat, 40
Neferty, 51
Neferusobek. *See* Nefrusobk
Nefrusobk, 11
Nekhbet, 14
Nemes, 14–15
Nephthys, 55, 79, 147
Nesmontu (general), 25
Neuserre, 78, 122
New Kingdom, 21, 72, 76, 83, 101;
    burial during, 39, 40; religion
    during, 138
Nile: canals of, 108–10; clay from, 69;
    fishing in, 126; flooding of, 2–3, 84,
    105–8, 116–17; low, 106–7; as
    transport link, 36–37
Nile-Hapy, 106
Nofret, 65
Nofret-iabet, *149*
Nomarchs, 9, 18–19
Nomes, 18–19
Novels, 49–51
Nubia, 8, 9, 11, 12, 23; colonists in,
    24–25; gold from, 92
Nubians, 8, 21, 28, 73
Nun, 139, 140

Nursing, of infants, 80
Nuu, 29, 133–34

Ogdoad, 140
Old Kingdom, 7–9, 14, 17, 85, 123–
    24; agricultural tools from, 107; art
    of, 59, 61–62, 65; children and
    families during, 77, 84; crafts
    during, 68–69, 71; daily life during,
    93, 95, 96; foreign policy during, 8,
    9, 21–23; irrigation during, 109,
    110; livestock farming during, 119,
    121–22; pyramids of, 7–8, 42;
    religion during, 8, 137–38, 142, 148,
    149–50. *See also specific dynasties*
"Opening of the mouth" ritual, 63,
    146
Ophois. *See* Wepwawet
Orchards, 116
Oryx nome, 106
Osiris, 7, 10, 137, 140, 147;
    epagomenal day of, 55; festivals of,
    142–43
Ostraca, 11, 46, 48

Painting, 47, 62–63, 107
Palaces, 16–17
Palestine, 8, 22, 25–26
Papyrus, 46, 48, 107–8, 131, 131–32
Pepy I, 8, 22, 28, 37
Pepy II, 8, 103–4
Pepy (official), 53
Peret, 3, 111–12
Pessimistic literature, 51–52
Pets, 83, 98–99
Pharaohs: foreign policy role of, 21;
    functions of statues of, 63; humanity
    of, 15–17; hunting by, 135–36; as
    landowners, 108; posthumous cult
    of, 149–50; and pyramid planning
    and construction, 40–41; as
    religious intermediary, 140–41;

statue at, 59; Wenis's pyramid at, 37, 68. *See also* Memphis

Saturn, 55

Scarabs, 93–94

Scheherazade, 51

Schist, 32–33

Science, 54–55; astronomy, 55–56; medicine, 56–57

Scorpion, 109

Scribes, *60, 109*; and cattle counts, 119–20; class status of, 10, 19–20, 45–46, 108; education of, 46–47, 53; materials used by, 47–49; outline, 62; as physicians, 56; and wisdom literature, 74

Sculpture, relief, 5, 61–62, 107. *See also* Statues

Seasons, 3, 55, 107–8, 111–14

Second Intermediate Period, 11

Sed-festival, 7, 15

Sehetepibre, 14

Seine fishing, *127, 127–28*

Sematawy, 10

Sementiu, 33

Semna, 24

Seneb. *See* Statues

Senebtisy, 28

Senedjemib, 40

Senet, 99

Senusert. *See* Senwosret

Senwosret, 110

Senwosret I, 15, 32, 141

Senwosret II, 25, 82, 85

Senwosret III, 11, 15, *16*, 143; foreign policy of, 21, 24

Serabit el-Khadim, 11, 36

Serra, 25

Seshat, 41

Sesostris. *See* Senwosret

Seth, 7, 55, 129–30, 133

Settlements, 1–2, 84–86, 87

Seven Wonders of the World, 8, 39

Sexuality, 78, 84

Shaduf, 110

Shahriyar, 51

Shaving, 88

"Sheikh el-Beled," 59

Shemu, 3, 112–14

Shepsesptah. *See* Ptahshepses

Shezemu, 83

Shipbuilding, 36–37, 67–68. *See also* Boats

Sinai, 7, 8, 21; mining in, 11, 29, 33, 34, 36

Sinuhe, 49–50, 76

Sirius, 3, 55

Sisene, 51

Sixth Dynasty, 8–9, 18, 22, 119, 145; architects during, 40; pottery during, 69; relief sculpture during, 61–62

Sledges, 30–32, *31*

Snofru, 8, 13, 40, 42, 67; benevolence of, 15

Sobek, 7, 129

Sobeknakhte, 80

Sokar, 7

Sothis (Sirius), 3, 55

Sphinxes, *xii*, 8, 14, *43*

Spinning, 71–72

Stadelmann, Rainer, 42

Statues, 59, 63–65; from cult of Hathor, 35; of Djehutihotpe, 30–31, *31*; of seated scribe, 60; of Seneb (Middle Kingdom), 64; of Seneb (Old Kingdom), *81*; of Senwosret III, *16*

Stoneware, 5, 6, 65–66, 97–98. *See also* Mines and quarries

Storehouses. *See* Granaries

Sudan, 100

Suez, 22

Sun disk, cult of, 138

Sunk relief, 62

Swamps. *See* Marshes
Syria, 8, 25, 147

Tales, 49–51
Tanning, 71
Taweret, 78
Taxes, 3, 9, 19, *109*
Tayt, 147
Tell el-Daba, 26
Temples, 8, 10, 63, 89, 138; of
   pharaohs, 42–43, 149–50;
   religious role of, 139–42
Tenth Dynasty, 15
Teti, 78, 101
Thebes (Luxor), 10, 12, 39, 107, 140
Thinite Period, 1, 7. *See also* First
   Dynasty
Third Dynasty, 7–8, 34, 36, 52, 145
Thirteenth Dynasty, 26
This, 7
Thoth, 10, 45
Thutmose. *See* Tuthmosis
Tombs: functions of, 144–45; of the
   poor, 73, 145; of Predynastic Era, 5,
   7; of pyramid construction workers,
   42; as research source, 11–12. *See
   also* Funerary beliefs; Mastabas;
   Pyramids
Tools, 5, 29, 65–66, 72, 89–90;
   agricultural, 107
Toys, 82–83
Trade, 8, 23, 25–26
Trades. *See* Crafts and trades
Transportation: by boat, 36–37,
   107–8; by litter, 98, 99; by sledge,
   30–32, *31*
Trapping, *125*, 125–26, 134
Treasury, 19
Trees, *116*
Tura, 36, 40, 41
Turquoise, 7, 11, 34, 36

Tuthmosis III, 121
Twelfth Dynasty, 10–11, 51, 80, 82;
   administrative reforms of, 10, 19–
   20; agriculture during, 109–10,
   111; foreign policy during, 24, 25–
   26; religion during, 141, 142
Ty, 98, 99, 122, 126, 127–28

Ukhhotep. *See* Wekh-hotpe
Unas. *See* Wenis
Unguents, 92
Upuaut. *See* Wepwawet
Usekh, 68–69, 93
Userkaf, 8
Ushabtis, 148
Uta, 71

Valley of the Kings, 39, 40, 137
Venus, 55
"Village Mayor," 59
Vineyards, *116*, 116–17
Viziers, 17–19, 27, 89. *See also
   specific viziers*

Wab priests, 141–42
Wadi el-Hudi, 33
Wadi Hammamat, 11, *30*, 32–33
Wadi Maghara, 36
Wadjit, 14
Wah, 146
Warfare, 8–9, 10, 11, 21–25
Washing, 87, 88–89
Watet-Khethor, 101
Weapons, 21–22, 26, 124–25, 130–
   31, 134
Weaving, 71–72, *72*, 89
Wekh-hotpe, 82
Weni (general), 22–23, 37
Wenis, 8, 37, 68
Wepwawet, 143

White Treasury, 19

Wigmaking, 91

Wine, 96, *116*, 116–17

Wisdom literature, 52–53, 74

Women: agricultural work of, 113–14; and childbirth, 78–79; clothing of, 89, *90*; craftwork of, 71–72, 73, 89; food preparation by, 95; hair of, 90, 91; literacy of, 49; marriage of, 74–77

Writing: hieratic script, 11, 45, 46, 150; origins of, 3–5. *See also* Hieroglyphic writing

Zatnebsekhtu, 54

INDEX TO TEXTS CITED